Funeral Service Business Law

A Guide for Funeral Service Students

Edward R. Mevec, JD

and

Larry J. Cleveland

Funeral Service Educators and Instructors

Licensed Funeral Directors

~ First Edition ~

First edition - June 2022

ISBN 978-1-736-6101-0-7

Published by Hudson Valley Professional Services
Queensbury, New York 12804
www.HudsonPros.com

Printed by Lightning Press
Totowa, New Jersey 07512
www.Lightning-Press.com

General Disclaimer - The material provided herein has been developed from several sources, including: state and federal statutory, administrative, and case law; government agency advisory opinions, bulletins, and administrative orders; knowledgeable instructors and practitioners in the funeral service; and information available to the general public in various communication mediums. The content of this book is believed to be accurate and true; however, practitioners should always consult an attorney for legal advice on any question of law in funeral service matters.

The opinions expressed in this publication are those of the authors. They do not reflect the opinions or views of any federal or state agency or official.

Table of Contents

PART 2: CONTRACTS

PART 3: SALES

PART 4: CONSUMER PROTECTIONS

PART 5: NEGOTIABLE INSTRUMENTS

PART 6: EMPLOYMENT

PART 7: BUSINESS ORGANIZATIONS

PART 8: PROPERTY LAW

PART 9: INSURANCE

Preface

Funeral service academic institutions across the United States provide students with the skills and knowledge they need to enter the workforce and successfully pursue their chosen profession. A significant portion of the material they study will deal with issues of regulatory compliance, as virtually every funeral event they encounter – from embalming human remains to meeting with families – will involve some level of compliance with federal, state, and/or local laws.

Regulatory compliance questions on the two-part National Board Examination (NBE) are developed from *specific* federal funeral service laws and *generic* state funeral service laws. There are no questions on the exam specific to a particular state or local government. Therefore, this book reviews in detail the federal statutes and their relationship to the funeral service industry, while also offering an overview and broad discussion of the more frequent and common requirements found across the nation in state and local statutes.

The content of this book has been identified by the American Board of Funeral Service Education (ABFSE) as being important in educating students about business law for funeral establishment, and this same ABFSE material is the foundation for the development of regulatory compliance questions on the NBE. This textbook provides both instructors and students with an up-to-date source of material designed to complement and enhance ABFSE educational mandates related to business law in general and – when appropriate – as it applies in the funeral service industry. The material is current, accurate, and essential to not only preparing future funeral directors for taking the NBE but for understanding regulatory compliance fundamentals they will be expected to follow throughout their careers as professional funeral service practitioners.

Edward R. Mevec
Larry J. Cleveland

Other Hudson Valley Professional Services Publications

Funeral Service Marketing & Merchandise
ISBN: 978-0-998-2571-2-9
Cleveland - January 2021

Funeral Directing in the United States 2E
ISBN: 978-1-736-6101-2-1
Cleveland - June 2022

Funeral Service Rites and Customs 2E
ISBN: 978-1-736-6101-3-8
Cleveland - June 2022

Funeral Service Law in the United States 2E
ISBN: 978-1-736-6101-1-4
Cleveland - June 2022

Cremation in the United States
ISBN: 978-0-998-2571-7-4
Cleveland - June 2021

Funeral Service Law in New York 2E
ISBN: 978-0-998-2571-9-8
Cleveland - January 2022

Book Introduction

Purpose and Intent

Purpose - The purpose of this textbook is to assist and promote funeral service students as they pursue a career in the funeral service industry, as well as to provide support to the college-level faculty and staff members serving as student mentors and classroom instructors. The book has been developed by incorporating and integrating the educational material identified by the American Board of Funeral Service Education (ABFSE) as being of importance to the subject of funeral service business law.

Intent - The intent of this textbook is to serve as a shared, common link between student and teacher; a link designed to serve both groups by presenting pertinent and relevant material in a consistent and organized style conducive to the learning environment. Integrating the information in this textbook with the skills and knowledge of the educator in the classroom is the formula to effectively preparing for and passing the two-part National Board Examination (NBE) at the conclusion of collegiate academic studies.

Use of Titles: Funeral Director, Undertaker, and Mortician

A cursory review of funeral service titles used by the fifty states reveals the vast majority have adopted the term *Funeral Director* to identify funeral service professionals. *Mortician* is still seen sporadically but now viewed by many within the service as sounding too morbid and gloomy. The term *Undertaker* is virtually non-existent, as state legislators have gradually phased this title out of the modern lexicon. Therefore, for the purposes of this book, the term *Funeral Director* is used to represent all three titles equally.

Use of the Terms: Requirement and Regulation

There are numerous federal and state laws, rules, regulations, and codes found in funeral service statutes and legislation; however, for the practitioner, the different terms are of no major importance when viewed from the perspective of regulatory compliance. In the interest of maintaining simplicity, the terms *requirement* and *regulation* are generally used to identify laws, rules, regulations, and codes at all levels of all governments. When important to bring context to a specific topic, a note is provided within the chapter text to further identify a legal source.

Definitions and Notes

Definitions - Where convenient for the reader, definitions are provided in the chapters and thereafter highlighted within the text with bold print. These definitions may also be repeated in subsequent chapters to provide prompt, easy access when of importance to the material being presented. All of the terms and definitions are compiled in a comprehensive glossary located in the back of the book.

Unless otherwise noted, the terms are definitions provided for use in accredited funeral service educational programs and therefore represent a potential source for test questions on the two-parts of the NBE. Some of the terms may be followed with a notation to identify their source from ABFSE glossaries, funeral service textbooks, legal statutes, research materials, the author, or other reliable authority. These notations and the sources they identify are as follows:

- FTC Guide - Information comes from the Federal Trade Commission publication titled, *Complying with the Funeral Rule*.

- [by Author] - Author provided definition of importance to understanding the material being presented.

- [CRM term] - *Cremation in the United States*, by Cleveland, © 2021.

- [FSL term] - *Funeral Service Law in the United States, 2nd ed.*, by Cleveland, © 2019.

- [SBM term] - ABFSE Small Business Management outline and glossary.

- [Oxford Dictionary] - Oxford University English Dictionary.

Notes - Notes are used in chapters to draw attention to material of specific interest or importance, or to provide additional clarification to a particular topic or subject of discussion. They are styled in the narrative as Note: with the additional information following immediately after the colon.

<u>Sources</u>

Sources of information are provided throughout the book and may be found in captions, annotations, or a specific attribution within the narrative. Each source includes the information or reference needed to quickly find it in the Sources Consulted section in the back of this book, where additional details and URLs (when available) are provided.

Chapter 1: Sources of Law in the United States

Overview
The information in this book is by design presented in a simplified format, free of complex narratives, stifling legal language, and administrative minutia. However, it is important for funeral service students and professionals alike to have a basic understanding of how laws, rules, and regulations are created and structured. This chapter addresses that need by exploring the various sources of law in the United States.

Chapter Definitions
Administrative agency - a governmental body created by legislation empowered to make and enforce rules and regulations.

Administrative law - the rules and regulations created by Federal and State administrative agencies.

Case law - appellate court decisions based on custom and usage and prior decisions.

Common law - the body of law deriving from judicial decisions, rather than from statutes or constitutions.

Constitution - the fundamental law that establishes the government; limits what government can and cannot do; and states the underlying principles to which the government will conform.

Funeral service law (mortuary law/mortuary jurisprudence) - that branch of law which relates to matters concerned with the disposal of the dead and regulation of funeral directors, embalmers, and funeral establishments.

Law - governmental rule prescribing conduct and carrying a penalty for violation.

Ordinance - law enacted by a local unit of government.

Police power - the inherent power of a government to make reasonable laws to protect the safety, health, morals, and general welfare of its citizens.

Rules and regulations - laws created by an administrative agency within its jurisdiction.

Stare decisis - the principle that the decision of a higher court should serve as a guide or precedent and control the decision of a similar case in the future.

Statutes - laws which are enacted by legislative bodies.

Introduction
Laws are government rules of conduct prescribing what is right and prohibiting what is wrong. The violation of a government law carries a penalty, most often in the form of a fine and/or incarceration. **Funeral service law** is that branch of law which relates to matters concerned with the disposal of the dead and the regulation of funeral directors, embalmers, and funeral establishments. Sources of funeral service law include federal and state constitutions, as well as

statutory and administrative laws developed by the three branches of our federal, state, and local governments – legislative, executive, and judicial. This chapter reviews these law sources:

Federal/state constitutions	Case law
Federal/state statutory laws	Common law
Municipal ordinances and laws	Administration law

Constitutions

A **constitution** is the fundamental law that establishes the government, limits what government can and cannot do, and states the underlying principles to which the government will conform.

Federal constitution - The powers contained in the Constitution of the United States – and those granted within the constitution to the three branches of our federal government – are the foundation upon which the individual federal codes, laws, rules, and regulations are developed and promulgated. The U.S. Constitution also provides checks and balances by and between the three branches by ensuring each has a role to play in writing, further defining, enforcing, and thereafter interpreting these laws. The laws found in the U.S. Constitution are superior to all other sources in both federal and state regulations and may only be superseded by amendment to the constitution, a complex and lengthy process.

State constitutions - Similar to the federal government, individual states have their own constitutions that provide the basis for *state* laws, rules, and regulations. Laws identified in a state constitution are superior to all other sources within the same state and may only be superseded by the Constitution of the United States.

Legislation (Statutory Law)

A **statute** is defined as a law enacted by a legislative body. At all government levels – federal, state, county, parish, city, town, and village – the legislative branch of the government passes legislation to create (write) statutory law. For example, state legislatures may pass laws that require a funeral director to be present and supervise the interment of human remains.

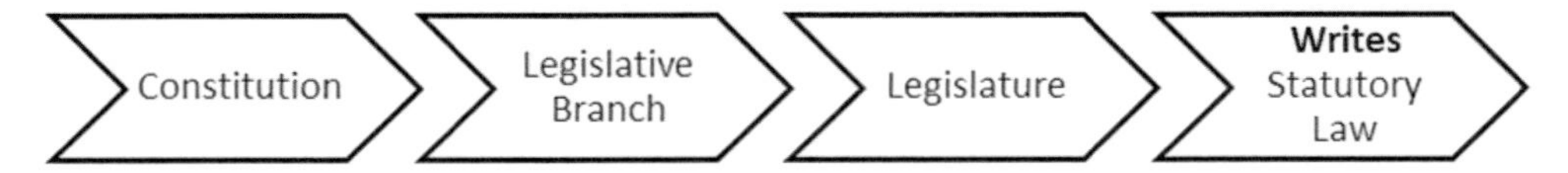

Federal statutory law - The legislative body in the United States is the U.S. Congress, as represented by two houses of government: the U.S. Senate and U.S. House of Representatives. Members of congress are elected by the citizens of their home state and sent to the government seat in Washington, D.C. to represent them. While in office, they carry out the duties afforded to them under the U.S. Constitution, including writing federal statutory laws initially known as bills.

Bills may undergo numerous iterations and changes as the two houses of Congress attempt to reconcile differences of opinion and strive to include provisions that best serve their constituents needs. Bills passed by Congress are sent to the President of the United States (a part of the executive branch of government) for approval or veto. If approved, they become statutory law, known as a United States Code (USC); if vetoed, they may never become law, or may become law if Congress can muster the necessary number of votes to override the veto. This process is all part of the checks and balances provided under the U.S. Constitution to ensure no one branch of government becomes excessively powerful.

A statutory law – written and passed by Congress – grants the Federal Trade Commission the authority to oversee government efforts to prevent unfair methods of competition. As will be explored in the administrative law section, this legislation was the genesis from which the Funeral Rule was born; this being the single, most important federal legislation to ever affect the funeral service industry in the United States.

State statutory law - State governments derive their authority to write laws based on the 10th Amendment to the U.S. Constitution. This amendment grants state governments **police power**, defined as the inherent power of a government to make reasonable laws to protect the safety, health, morals, and general welfare of its citizens. State statutes may regulate such areas as:

- the licensing of funeral service professionals;
- defining the parameters for owning and operating a funeral service business;
- setting minimum workplace standards for funeral service employees;
- establishing business practices to provide for consumer protections; and
- creating minimum standards that govern the health care community.

Using the police power granted to them by the U.S. Constitution, the legislatures of the 50 states write and pass statutory law in a fashion similar to the federal government, although the names of their legislative bodies and the procedures they follow vary from one state to the next. State laws that affect funeral directing activities – such as contract law and probate law – are in addition to those existing in federal statutes but of equal importance to the funeral service professional.

Note: In 27 states, the state legislative body is called a legislature or state legislature; in 19 states, a general assembly; in Massachusetts and New Hampshire, a general court; and, in North Dakota and Oregon, a legislative assembly.

Municipal local laws - Government municipalities, such as counties, parishes, cities, towns, and villages may write laws specific to their communities. This is usually accomplished through a municipal board, council, or legislature. The laws they pass may be known as **ordinances**, defined as laws passed by a local municipal governing body (e.g., zoning, building, safety, etc.). They may also be known as local laws in certain states.

For example, a town government may pass a zoning *ordinance* that lists the building and construction zones where a funeral establishment may be erected and operated; while a county government may pass a *local law* to regulate the duties and activities of a county coroner or medical examiner.

Case Law

Having determined the legislative branches of government write statutory law, the focus now turns to the role played by the judicial branches of government, the branches tasked with *interpreting* those laws. Appellate courts in the judicial branch are responsible for hearing appeals from cases that have already been heard in trial (lower) courts. The decisions they render become **case law**, defined as appellate court decisions based on custom and usage and prior decisions.

Decision making - When questions of law come before a court for interpretation, the court gathers information from a wide range of sources and applies established legal principles to assist them in the decision-making process, including:

- written briefs (narratives and summaries) from the parties involved;
- sworn testimony of relevance to the issue under consideration;
- legislative records, which often contain insight on the intent and purpose of lawmakers that prompted them to write the relevant statutory law under review by the court;
- administrative agency records, which often contain background information on the reasoning and motive behind any rules and regulations under review;
- prior rulings and decisions of a higher court on similar matters that serve as an example to resolve future similar cases (known as case precedents);
- adhering to the principle of **stare decisis**, which provides for a court to stand by a decision and apply it to future cases where the facts are substantially the same; and
- existing common law rulings, decisions, and opinions.

Federal courts - The federal court system has three levels:

- district courts (the trial courts);
- courts of appeal, which are the first level of appeal; and
- the Supreme Court of the United States, the highest level of appeal in the federal system.

State courts - State court structures vary slightly but generally follow a pattern similar to the federal court system. They have one or more levels of trial courts where cases originate; and one or more levels of appellate courts where decisions rendered by the trial courts may be appealed by the parties involved.

Note: For additional information on judicial systems, see the chapter titled, *The Judicial System*.

Common Law

Unlike a statutory law, with its origin easily traced to the legislative branch of a government, **common law** finds its roots in the judicial branch. The law is derived from the court review of custom, practice, judicial rulings and decisions, and established case law. Because of this close affiliation with the judicial branch, it is often called judge-made law. Common law may be encountered by funeral service practitioners, especially when making a determination on who has a priority right to control the final disposition of human remains.

For example, consider a man who wants to make funeral arrangements for his deceased wife. They were together for 46 years; have four children and nine grandchildren; owned a home together; and shared all of the common attributes of a husband and wife. The only issue is they were never actually married in a civil proceeding, and the state statute provides a 'spouse' has the priority right to control the funeral.

In similar cases, judges have consistently viewed this from the perspective of long-standing custom and practice, which would demonstrate – but for the lack of a civil wedding – the couple were in a common law marriage and equally entitled to the rights and privileges bestowed on a civilly married husband and wife. The wife would be considered – for all reasonable purposes – the spouse. There may be no statutory law that spells out this position, but by exercising the power and authority of the court, common law has been established to support this position.

Note: Many states have proactively addressed the issue presented in the previous example by changing statutory law to provide for a 'domestic partner' to have the next priority right to control a disposition following a 'spouse' when no spouse exists.

Administrative Law

As stated earlier, all three government branches – legislative, executive, and judicial – play a role in writing, further defining, enforcing, and interpreting laws. The review up to this point has focused on the power of the legislative branch to *write* statutory law and the judicial branch to *interpret* statutory law. The focus now turns to the contributions made by the executive branch.

The executive branch of government exercises authority through **administrative agencies**, such as commissions, departments, divisions, bureaus, and offices by giving them rule-making power and authority. These administrative agencies *further define and reinforce* statutory laws by adopting **rules and regulations** and issuing opinions, orders, and decisions. Administrative agencies are also charged with the enforcement of administrative laws, rules, and regulations, with all of these activities coming under the heading of **administrative law**.

Federal administrative laws - In order to ensure a statutory law meets the intended purpose for which it was passed, federal administrative agencies routinely undertake a wide range of activities to further define and reinforce the provisions. These actions – and the written rules and regulations they develop – create the federal administrative laws they are then charged with enforcing.

For example, the *Prevention of Unfair Methods of Competition* statute, written by Congress and found in USC Title 15, gave the Federal Trade Commission (an administrative agency) the power and authority to issue a rule to regulate Funeral Industry Practices. This rule – now known informally as the Funeral Rule – may be found in the Code of Federal Rules (CFR).

In addition to formal rules, administrative agencies often issue guidelines, opinions, and decisions. In the case of the Federal Trade Commission and the Funeral Rule, the agency has issued several advisory opinions on the purchase, delivery, and use of so-called third-party caskets; caskets purchased from an entity other than the funeral establishment providing all of the other goods and services for a funeral. These opinions are only advisory in nature but often become a part of the rule when next revised. The issue of third-party caskets is addressed further in following chapters.

State administrative laws - All 50 states have administrative agencies that create and actively enforce administrative laws, rules, and regulations to further define and reinforce state statutes. The titles of the official compilations of state administrative laws vary state to state but are usually readily recognizable, as shown in this table

Regulations of **Connecticut** State Agencies	Rules and Regulations of the State of **Georgia**	**New York** Codes, Rules and Regulations
Code of **Rhode Island** Rules	Code of **Colorado** Regulations	**Texas** Administrative Code

In most states, there is a bureau or office under the umbrella of a health department that oversees the funeral service industry. These agencies write rules to provide for such things as the licensure of funeral service professionals; ownership and operation of funeral service establishments; and acceptable practices in funeral service, such as the removal, transfer, and transportation of human remains within the state.

In Summary

As has been explored in this chapter, there are a number of law sources in the United States spread across all three branches of federal, state, and local governments. At times, this becomes problematic for the funeral service professional trying to find an answer to a particular legal question, given the fact several sources may need to be consulted to arrive at a conclusive answer. However, this situation is not unique to the funeral service. In fact, this is the very reason businesses of every design often need an attorney to render legal advice and opinions.

Chapter 2: Bodies of Law

Overview

There are two major bodies of law in the United States: criminal law, also known as public law; and civil law, also known as private law. This chapter explores what distinguishes these two bodies apart from each other in the American jurisprudence system.

Chapter Definitions

Adjudicate - the process of rendering a formal decision or judgment in a matter that is in dispute or adversarial in nature.

Business law - rules of conduct for the performance of business transactions.

Case law - appellate court decisions based on custom and usage and prior decisions.

Civil law - the body of law concerned with private or purely personal rights.

Common law - the body of law deriving from judicial decisions, rather than from statutes or constitutions.

Crime - an offense which is injurious to society as a whole.

Criminal law - laws dealing with crimes and the punishment of wrongdoers.

Felony - serious criminal offense punishable by imprisonment for more than one year or death.

Law - governmental rule prescribing conduct and carrying a penalty for violation.

Misdemeanor - a less serious crime punishable by fine and/or imprisonment of less than one year.

Negligence - failure to exercise reasonable care.

Police power - the inherent power of a government to make reasonable laws to protect the safety, health, morals, and general welfare of its citizens.

Statutes - laws which are enacted by legislative bodies.

Tort - a private or civil wrong against a person or his or her property, other than by breach of contract, for which there may be action for damages.

Common Law - Historically

Common law is a legal term that has more than one meaning, although all have similar elements. When used to identify the organization and structure of jurisprudence in the United States, common law is described as a legal system that originated in England and was brought to the United States by the British colonists when they first settled in America. Common law – as a system – was the historical foundation of American law.

West's Encyclopedia of American Law describes 'common law' as:

> *The ancient law of England based upon societal customs and recognized and enforced by the judgments and decrees of the courts. The general body of statutes and case law that governed England and the American colonies prior to the American Revolution.*
>
> *The principles and rules of actions, embodied in case law rather than legislative enactments, applicable to the government and protection of persons and property that derive their authority from the community customs and traditions that evolved over the centuries as interpreted by judicial tribunals.*

Common law, within the common law system used in the United States, is defined as a body of law derived from the court review of custom, practice, and judicial rulings and decisions, rather than from statutes or constitutions. The term is similar to, and often used interchangeably with, **case law**, defined as appellate court decisions based on custom, usage, and prior decisions. And lastly, as noted in the previous chapter, it may be referred to informally as judge-made law.

<u>Criminal Law vs. Civil Law</u>

Broadly, the purpose of **criminal law** is to protect society as a whole, while the purpose of **civil law** is to provide remedies for an individual that has been subjected to an act or omission by another that results in an injury or harm. The difference between the two bodies of law is not always a bright line, as a crime against the public (society) is also often an act against an individual that causes them injury or harm.

For example, if a person attacks and assaults another person causing them physical injury, the attacker could be arrested under criminal law statutes for an offense against the public as a whole, even though the actual victim is an individual member of the public. In addition, the victim could use the provisions afforded to them in civil law to seek restitution and compensation for the injuries they sustained from the assailant.

West's Encyclopedia of American Law describes 'criminal law' and 'civil law' as follows:

> *– Criminal Law*
>
> *A body of rules and statutes that defines conduct prohibited by the government because it threatens and harms **public** safety and welfare and that establishes punishment to be imposed for the commission of such acts.* [**Bold** emphasis added]
>
> *– Civil Law*
>
> *A body of rules that delineate **private** rights and remedies, and govern disputes between individuals in such as areas as contracts, property, and family law; distinct from criminal or public law.* [**Bold** emphasis added]

Criminal Law

Police power is the inherent power of a government to make reasonable laws to protect the safety, health, morals, and general welfare of its citizens. This includes criminal laws (**statutes**) initially passed by the legislative branch of government. These laws are then enforced by the executive branch and interpreted by the judicial branch as needed before being **adjudicated**. The primary goal of having criminal laws is the protection of the public-at-large. To achieve this goal, criminal laws serve many functions, including:

- giving fair notice of unacceptable conduct that creates an offense against the public;
- defining legal parameters for the arrest and prosecution of an offender;
- setting the penalties to punish those who are convicted of committing crimes;
- promoting programs for the correction and rehabilitation of offenders;
- serving as a deterrent to others to not engage in criminal conduct; and
- preventing **crime**.

Criminal laws define the conduct a government considers to be threating or harmful to the health, safety, property, and moral welfare of society. The laws the government passes are collectively called offenses and most often separated into two major categories: crimes and petty offenses. Each of these are then further divided into classifications.

Crimes

Crimes are offenses for which a person may be punished by a period of imprisonment or incarceration in a government facility. When operated by the federal government, these facilities are known as penitentiaries; when a state government, prisons; and when a local government, a jail or lockup.

A person arrested for a criminal offense will have their fingerprints and picture taken. In some states, they may have a blood or saliva sample taken to obtain a DNA profile. If convicted of the crime for which they were arrested, they will be a criminal – a label that has life-long implications, including such things as not being permitted to own or possess a firearm, engage in certain occupations, or obtain a passport. They also may face social stigma within the community that makes it difficult to attain simple life needs, such as rent an apartment or find a job.

Felony - A **felony** is a serious criminal offense punishable by imprisonment for over one year. The distinction of imprisonment for more than one year is significant, in that terms of more than one year are usually spent in a state prison rather than a local jail or lockup. This may remove the convicted criminal to a far distant location away from family and friends. Felonies are usually given letter classifications, such as a class B felony, and may in some states also have numeric sub-classifications, such as a class C-1 felony. Some states prohibit convicted felons from being licensed funeral directors.

Misdemeanor - A **misdemeanor** is a less serious crime punishable by a fine and/or imprisonment of less than one year in a local facility. Nonetheless, a conviction for a misdemeanor is still a criminal conviction that has similar implications to having been convicted of a felony. Misdemeanors have letter classifications and may in some states have numeric sub-classifications. Several states have an 'unclassified misdemeanor' as a default classification in those cases where a particular criminal statute or law does not specifically state a letter classification.

For example, the state of Arkansas uses this language to address unclassified misdemeanors:

> *If a criminal statute states that the crime is a misdemeanor but does not place a limitation on the sentence or otherwise classify the misdemeanor, the crime is presumed to be a Class A misdemeanor.* [Source: Arkansas Code § 5-4-401]

Other penalties - In addition to imprisonment, penalties found in some states may include:

fines	boot camps[1]	community supervision	asset forfeiture	probation
house arrest	death	community service	scarlet letters[2]	parole

[1] Boot camps are military style barracks where young, first-time offenders undergo rigorous physical and behavioral training for three to six months designed to instill discipline and hold youths accountable for their actions.

[2] Scarlet letter is punishment by shaming, such as a court ordering a child molester to put out a yard sign announcing their crime, or ordering a drunk driver to put bright orange bumper stickers on their vehicle that urge other drivers to report any erratic operation to police.

Petty Offenses

Petty offenses are non-criminal offenses, including violations and traffic infractions. When a person is charged with a petty offense, there is no fingerprinting, mugshot, or collection of a DNA sample. If convicted of a petty offense, the offender has not been convicted of a crime and does not have a criminal record.

Violations - This sub-classification of petty offenses prohibits certain conduct or behavior, including such activities as disorderly conduct, harassment, trespassing, and loitering. Typical punishments for a violation include monetary fines, community service and, when applicable, restitution for any damage or loss to others. A person convicted of a violation may be sentenced to a minimal number of days in a local jail or lockup, but incarceration is not the norm for petty offenses, especially for first-time offenders and adolescents.

Traffic infractions - Such offenses as speeding, running a red light, and passing a stopped school bus are typical traffic infractions. As petty offenses, they are considered minor in nature. Monetary fines are the predominant punishment, followed by suspension or revocation of driving privileges for repetitive convictions. Certain traffic-related conduct, such as driving under the influence of alcohol or drugs are classified as crimes.

Civil Law

Civil law is the body of law concerned with private or purely personal rights. It deals with relationships between individuals and the duties imposed upon them by law. For example, a funeral establishment has an inherent duty to provide for the safeguarding, care, preparation, and final disposition of human remains. If the survivors of the decedent believe they suffered some form of harm or injury because a funeral director did not meet their duty to provide an appropriate level of care, a civil claim could be filed in a civil court. The civil law system is adversarial, with a judge or other judicial official moderating between two opposing parties. In this example, the family and the funeral home would be adversaries going before a judge or other court official.

The most common types of civil complaints filed in civil courts are those that involve contract, property, or tort offenses.

Torts

A **tort** is a private or civil wrong against a person or his or her property, other than by breach of contract, for which there may be action for damages. The Cornell Law School Legal Information Institute defines a tort as an:

> *... act or omission that gives rise to injury or harm to another and amounts to a civil wrong for which courts impose liability. In the context of torts, injury describes the invasion of any legal right, whereas harm describes a loss or detriment in fact that an individual suffers.*

There are three basic types of torts:

1. *Intentional* - Exists when an individual knowingly and intentionally engages in conduct with the intended result that another will suffer some form of damage or loss.

2. *Negligent* - Exists when an individual carelessly or negligently engages in conduct that results in an unintentional damage or loss to another. This type of tort has many potential sources, including failure to exercise due care (**negligence**), dereliction of duty, failure to perform a required or promised duty, carelessness, and inattentiveness.

3. *Strict liability* - Provides an individual or entity may be held liable for their conduct without the need to prove the act was either intentional or negligent. This type of tort is often associated with product liability, such as when a consumer purchases a product that is later determined to be defective or faulty in design.

Tort claims - Tort claims are filed in civil courts as opposed to criminal courts. They represent an action taken by one party (such as a family member) to pursue compensation for an injury or loss they believe was the result of an act or omission by another party (such as a funeral director).

The owner or operator of a funeral establishment has certain obligations, duties, and responsibilities that may include such items as:

- ➢ their primary duty of providing for the safeguarding, care, preparation, and final disposition of human remains;

- ➢ the responsibility to properly dispose of potentially infectious waste in a manner that protects public health and safety;

- a duty to operate and maintain facilities and grounds in conformity with regulatory requirements to provide a safe environment for consumers, visitors, and employees;
- the responsibility to comply with the Americans with Disabilities Act by providing for handicapped access to the facilities; and
- a duty and obligation to comply with OSHA standards to provide a safe work environment for employees performing tasks in a preparation room or morgue facility.

If a funeral establishment owner or operator fails to meet any of these duties, responsibilities, or obligations – especially as they relate to activities dealing with the care and preparation of human remains – they may be subject to a civil claim.

Contract Law

A contract is defined as a legally enforceable agreement. There are four essential elements that make up a legally enforceable contract:

1. An offer - a proposal to make a contract.
2. An acceptance - an agreement to an offer.
3. Contractual capacity - the legal ability to enter into a contract.
4. Consideration - the bargained-for exchange in a contract.

If the terms of a contract are broken (breached), an aggrieved party may file a civil claim to seek restitution and compensation for damages. A breach of contract is not a tort because in a tort claim there is a duty imposed by law that has been violated, not a breach of an agreement or contract between the parties. In contract law, the duty is found in the agreement or contract, not the law.

Business Law

The rules of conduct for the performance of business transactions is the definition of **business law**. It includes laws that pertain to starting or acquiring a business and the management and operation of the business. Business laws may be found in all government levels – federal, state, and local. For example, the federal government enforces the Funeral Rule and state governments regulate the licensing and registration of funeral directors.

Property Law

Property law regulates the ownership of property, including real property and personal property. It includes the rights of those who own property; requirements for the sale, transfer, or other disposition of property; and the means to settle claims against property.

Note: Contract law and property law are explored in detail in later chapters.

Chapter 3: The Judicial Process

Overview

The judicial branches of our governments oversee the legal matters that come before our courts. Whether they are related to a civil law or criminal law case, the courts follow established procedures and rules to ensure the judicial process treats all persons equally and impartially while maintaining dignity and decorum.

This chapter explores federal and state court systems, and concludes with a hypothetical case to demonstrate how a civil court proceeding would progress if a lawsuit were to be filed against a funeral establishment and/or a funeral director.

Chapter Definitions

Answer - official document responding to the plaintiff's complaint.

Appeal - request to a higher court to review a lower court's decision.

Appellate courts - courts hearing cases appealed from a lower court.

Complaint (petition) - the document which initiates a civil lawsuit.

Defendant - the party against whom legal action is brought.

Discovery - the formal and informal exchange of information between sides in a lawsuit.

Execution - the carrying out or completion of some task.

Impeach - call into question the integrity or validity of (a practice) [Oxford Dictionary].

Judgment - a decision of a court.

Jurisdiction - the official power to make legal decisions and judgments [Oxford Dictionary].

Perjury - offense of willfully telling an untruth in a court after having taken an oath or affirmation [Oxford Dictionary].

Plaintiff - the party who initiates a civil action.

Probate court - a court having jurisdiction over estates.

Summons - a notice given to a defendant, attaching the complaint and stating a time frame in which to respond.

Trial court - court which conducts the original trial of a case.

Jurisdiction

The Oxford English Dictionary defines **jurisdiction** as the official power to make legal decisions and **judgments**. The various courts derive their jurisdiction, power, and authority by means of the United States Constitution and the constitutions of the states. These courts make legal decisions and render judgments within the geographical areas over which they have jurisdiction.

Trial courts - A **trial court** is one in which a case originates or initially comes before a judge. For example, if a funeral director were to have a civil claim filed against them by a family member of a decedent, the filing would take place in a trial court. The funeral director and the family member would go before a trial court judge who would preside over the case and serve as a moderator between the parties. Trial courts are often referred to as a court of original jurisdiction, as this is where a case originates when a lawsuit if first filed.

Appellate courts - Parties to a case in a trial court may have the right to **appeal** a decision of the court by taking the case up to an appellate level court. An **appellate court** hears cases appealed from a lower court. The lower court may be a trial court or a lower-level appellate court than the one to which the appeal has been filed. In the above example, if a judge or jury ruled in favor of the funeral director, the family member may be allowed to appeal the ruling to an appellate court, in which case the parties would then go before an appellate court judge or panel of judges.

Federal Court System

The federal court system has three levels:

1. District Courts - The nation's 94 district or general trial courts are called U.S. District Courts and are overseen by District Judges. These courts resolve disputes by determining the facts, applying legal principles, and rendering decisions. Trial courts include a district judge who oversees the case and a jury that decides the case. Magistrate judges assist district judges in preparing cases for trial and may also conduct trials in misdemeanor matters. There is at least one district court in each state and the District of Columbia.

2. Courts of Appeals - There are 13 appellate courts, collectively called the U.S. Courts of Appeals and widely known as circuit courts. An appellate court hears challenges to decisions from the district courts located within its circuit (jurisdiction). The task of the appellate court is to determine whether or not the law was applied correctly in the trial court. Appeals courts consist of three judges and do not use a jury. The 94 federal district courts are organized into 12 regional circuits, each of which has a court of appeals identified by the regional circuit where they are located.

3. Supreme Court - The Supreme Court is of course the highest court in the United States. It has appellate jurisdiction over all federal and state cases involving federal laws and original jurisdiction in certain specific circumstances, such as any case in which a state is one of the parties. As a part of the checks and balances on the three branches of government, the Supreme Court has the authority to rule on the constitutionality and lawfulness of directives issued by the president.

State Court Systems

State court structures and systems vary slightly but generally follow a pattern similar to the federal courts. They may have one or more levels of trial courts where cases originate; and one or more levels of appellate courts where decisions rendered by the trial courts may be appealed. Some states categorize the trial courts as inferior courts and the appellate courts as superior courts.

With two exceptions, the highest court in each of the 50 states is named a Supreme Court. The two exceptions – New York and Maryland – named their highest court a Court of Appeals. Whenever the highest court in a state renders a decision, the ruling becomes the superior authority – law of the land – applicable to all subordinate courts in the home state, subject only to any decisions and case laws of the United States Supreme Court on the same issue.

Similar to federal courts, state systems have courts with jurisdiction over special types of cases. For example, the process of administering an estate and determining the validity of a will is supervised by a **probate court,** the name most often associated with a court having jurisdiction over estates in the United States. However, there are states that assign probate duties to a court of a different name, such as the Superior Court in California; Court of Chancery in Delaware; and Surrogate's Court in New Jersey. Probate courts also supervise the administration of estates for cases where the decedent did not have a will at the time of death.

Submitting a Court Action

The opening page on documents prepared for filing with a criminal or civil court to commence an action include a caption that identifies the names of the parties, the name of the court, the court case number, and the title or type of action being submitted.

Criminal court actions - A crime is an offense for conduct which is injurious to society as a whole, and the conduct is prohibited by the government because it threatens and harms *public* safety and welfare. As such, the parties in the caption on a criminal case list the people of the state or municipality as the charging party; and the person against whom criminal action is brought as the **defendant**.

This is the Portion of a Criminal Charge Caption that IDs the Parties

==

The People of the State of Arkansas

-vs-

Hudson Michael Valley

defendant

==

Some states, such as Minnesota, further identify the charging party as being the **plaintiff**, generally known as the party that initiates a court action and more often seen in civil action captions. The use of the word 'against' is also used by some states rather than the abbreviation for versus.

Civil court actions - Again from the previous chapter, civil law is described as the body of law concerned with *private* or purely personal rights. It deals with relationships between individuals and the duties imposed upon them by law. As such, the parties in the caption on a civil case list the individual(s) making the complaint; and the individual(s) against whom the complaint is being brought.

This is the Portion of a Civil Complaint Caption that IDs the Parties

==

William M. Baker
Mary J. Baker *plaintiffs*
- against -

Smith Funeral Home
Michael Smith *defendants*

==

The parties to this civil case are the two plaintiffs, William Baker and Mary Baker, filing a civil action (lawsuit) against two defendants, the Smith Funeral Home and the funeral director, Michael Smith, who owns and operates the establishment.

Civil Court Process and Procedures - Case Example

The discussion that follows uses a hypothetical civil case to highlight the key procedures in a civil court claim. The case is as follows:

> Michael Smith, a funeral director and owner/operator of the Smith Funeral Home, handled arrangements and provided funeral goods and services to the family of Robert Green following his death. Mr. Green's wife, Susan Green, was the person with the priority right to control the final disposition of his remains, and she selected the goods and services for the funeral service events.
>
> When the casket was being carrying to the grave by the bearers for an interment service, the bottom suddenly – and with no warning – broke loose, and the decedent fell out of the casket and onto the ground with a loud thud in front of everyone gathered for the interment service. Screaming could be heard for miles.

The complaint - A civil action is commenced in court by the initial filing of a civil **complaint**, sometimes known as a petition, by one or more plaintiffs against one or more defendants.

West's Encyclopedia of American Law describes the purpose of a civil complaint as follows:

> *A civil complaint initiates a civil lawsuit by setting forth for the court a claim for relief from damages caused, or wrongful conduct engaged in, by the defendant. The complaint outlines all of the plaintiff's theories of relief, or causes of action*

(e.g., negligence, battery, assault), and the facts supporting each cause of action. The complaint also serves as notice to the defendant that legal action is underway.

A plaintiff may be called a complainant or petitioner in some jurisdictions, but the titles all serve the same purpose of identifying who has initialed a civil case against another party in a court of law. In the Smith case, Susan Green hired a lawyer to sue the funeral home and the funeral director for emotional suffering, mental anguish, and psychological injury from her witnessing the remains of her husband being dropped onto the ground. Susan is therefore the plaintiff and the funeral home and funeral director are defendants.

The summons - A **summons** is a written notice – usually with a complaint attached – that is given to a defendant. A summons states a time frame in which the defendant must respond. The purpose of a summons and complaint is to serve legal notice to a defendant that a case is being filed against them that needs to resolved in a court of law.

In most cases, a summons and complaint must be served on the defendant – or the defendants' attorney – to provide proof they were given adequate notice of the civil claim. The most prevalent method of service is called personal service and requires the documents be given personally and directly to the defendant. Substitute or mail service methods are acceptable in limited circumstances but can sometimes present issues in establishing the defendant did in fact receive the summons.

A summons requires a plaintiff to participate in the legal process and may include any of these additional stipulations or directives:

- a directive to appear at a scheduled legal hearing, deposition, or proceeding;
- a requirement to submit relevant records or documentation to the plaintiff;
- a response, or **answer**, to the allegations made in the complaint; and/or
- a personal appearance before a judge.

If a funeral director or other representative of a funeral establishment is served with or receives a civil summons, it is important they promptly seek legal counsel to avoid the possibility of missing any court imposed deadlines for submissions or required appearances.

The answer - An answer is the official document prepared by the defendant(s) in response to a plaintiff's complaint.

West's Encyclopedia of American Law describes an answer to a complaint as follows:

> *Answer*
> *The first responsive pleading filed by the defendant in a civil action; a formal written statement that admits or denies the allegations in the complaint and sets forth any affirmative defenses.*

An answer to the claims made in a lawsuit must be submitted within a set number of days and may include any affirmative defenses – facts that are presented to defeat claims made in the complaint even if the claims are factually correct.

Typical Statement in a Summons that Requires an Answer from the Defendant

You are hereby summoned and required to answer the Complaint in this action, a copy of which is herewith served upon you, and to serve a copy of your answer to the Complaint on the subscriber at his office, Robert A. Smith, Esq., P.O. Box 123, Macon, NZ, 12345, within twenty (20) days after the service hereof (or within thirty (30) days after the service is complete if this summons is not personally delivered to you), exclusive of the day of such service, and if you fail to answer the complaint within the time aforesaid, the Plaintiff in this action will apply to the court for the relief demanded in the Complaint.

Discovery - One might think the next step in the judicial process would be to have a trial. However in practice the process is just beginning, and there is much more work to be done before going to trial. In fact, relatively few civil cases ever do go to trial because the parties – after exchanging information with each other – decide to settle the case.

The American Bar Association has stated:

> *Relatively few lawsuits ever go through the full range of procedures and all the way to trial. Most civil cases are settled by mutual agreement between the parties. A dispute can be settled even before a suit is filed. Once a suit is filed, it can be settled before the trial begins, during the trial, while the jury is deliberating, or even after a verdict is rendered.*

The exchange of information between the parties is known as **discovery** – a pre-trial process that takes place according to established civil law practice and procedures. The purpose of discovery is to provide a means for all of the parties to become fully acquainted with the facts and circumstances of the case. Discovery may take the form of depositions, evidence, and interrogatories.

Depositions - These are formal sessions in which a person – called a deponent – is questioned under oath about information or knowledge they have relevant to a case. The purpose is to find out what they actually know about the case and have their sworn testimony documented. Michael Smith is the funeral director that sold the casket that failed and could be required to sit for a deposition. Because the construction of the casket will be a central point in this case, he may be asked to answer inquiries about:

- his understanding of the Magnuson-Moss Warranty Act law as it relates to implied warranties and warranty disclaimers;
- his understanding of the funeral home policy on providing consumers with product warranty information;

- what, if anything, he told the family at the time of the sale about casket warranties in general, and the casket purchased for the funeral in particular;
- his past experience and knowledge in casket construction and components; and
- if he is aware of any similar failed casket incidents in either his funeral home or any other funeral home businesses.

Evidence - Either party may request the production of physical evidence related to the case. These requests usually pertain to documents and records, although other tangible evidence items may be requested. In this case, the evidence requested may include:

- records about the purchase of the casket from the manufacturer and subsequent sale to Susan Green;
- warranty information available from the manufacturer or distributor of the casket;
- brochures, pamphlets, or other documents meant for distribution to consumers that describe the casket;
- copy of the FTC mandated casket price list in effect on the day of the casket purchase;
- internal business records about any similar casket failures; and
- requesting the damaged casket be made available for an independent inspection or examination by an expert in casket construction.

Interrogatories - These are written questions that require the person answering them to swear an oath or affirm to a notary, under penalty of **perjury**, their responses are true and accurate. They are often designed to identify information and areas to be further explored or examined in preparing for a trial. In this case, questions might read something similar to these two examples:

- Identify every person who has, or may have, any knowledge or facts regarding this matter, and state the substance of their knowledge.
- Identify the education, training, and experience of the named defendant, Michael Smith, as it relates to his occupation as a funeral director.

Both sworn testimony at a deposition and sworn answers to interrogatories may be used during a trial or other formal hearing to challenge – and thereby **impeach** – a witness that is changing their testimony during the trial from what they stated at the deposition or answered in an interrogatory. A witness may be impeached if proof can be submitted to establish they contradicted themselves in acts or statements inconsistent with the sworn testimony being given in a court proceeding.

Trial - If the parties to a civil action cannot come to an agreement among themselves and settle the case, it may then go to a trial. During a trial, the plaintiffs, defendants, witnesses, and experts may be called to testify by direct examination in a courtroom and under oath. In most civil matters, a jury trial is available to the defendant, but there are some state provisions that limit access to a jury based on the compensation being sought or the nature of the alleged harm or injury. In those cases where a jury is not allowed or required, a *trial by judge* may be the forum.

At the conclusion of a civil trial, the jury or judge (as the case may be) evaluates the testimony and evidence presented and renders a finding in favor of either the plaintiff or the defendant.

If they find in favor of the defendant (person sued), the case is dismissed.

If they find in favor of the plaintiff (person suing), a jury or judge may then award monetary damages to be paid by the defendant to the plaintiff.

Awards may be in the form of *compensatory* damages, to compensate the plaintiff for any damages, injuries, or loss; and/or *punitive* damages, to punish the defendant for the conduct that caused the harm or injury.

Execution - Also known in some states as a writ of execution, an **execution** is a court order directing a sheriff or other law enforcement official to take possession of property from the defendant to satisfy (pay) a judgment when the defendant has not voluntarily done so as ordered by the court.

These execution orders most often direct the seizure of money and assets from a defendants' bank accounts, which funds are then remitted (paid) to the plaintiff. There are federal and state exemptions to what property may be taken with an execution. For example, a defendants' income from programs administered by the Social Security Administration are exempt from seizure.

Chapter 4: Classification of Contracts

Overview

Funeral directors enter into a contractual agreement when consumers purchase – and funeral directors agree to furnish – merchandise and services. It is therefore important to understand what a contract is and the types of contracts that are a part of everyday life. This chapter identifies and reviews the various types of oral and written contracts.

Chapter Definitions

Acceptance - an agreement to any offering resulting in a contract.

Bilateral contract - a contract which consists of mutual promises to perform future acts.

Consideration - the bargained-for exchange in a contract.

Contract - a legally enforceable agreement.

Contractual capacity - the legal ability to enter into an agreement.

Executed contract - a contract in which the terms have been fulfilled.

Executory contract - A contract in which the terms have not been completely executed or fulfilled.

Express contract - a contract in which the parties express their intentions, either verbally or in writing, at the time of the agreement.

Fiduciary - a person in a relationship of trust and confidence.

Implied contract - one in which the terms of the contract are implied by acts or conduct of the parties.

Offer - a proposal to make a contract.

Oral contract - one that has been agreed to but not fully reduced to writing; and a written contract as one where the terms have been reduced to writing

Quasi contract - a contract created or implied by law to prevent unjust enrichment.

Real property - land and those objects permanently attached to the land.

Statute of Frauds - law requiring certain contracts be in writing to be enforceable.

Unenforceable contract - an agreement which is not in the form required by law.

Uniform Commercial Code - model act that includes provisions concerning certain sales of goods and negotiable instruments.

Unilateral contract - a contract formed when an act is done in consideration for a promise.

Valid contract - a contract which is legally enforceable.

Void contract - an agreement of no legal effect.

Voidable contract - a contract which would be an enforceable agreement, but due to circumstances may be set aside by one of the parties.

Contracts

A **contract** is defined as a legally enforceable agreement. Seems simple enough. Unfortunately, a contract it is not as simple as the definition because the United States does not have a vast body of contract law that provides uniform rules for the use of these important documents. Contract law is in fact varied and fact intensive.

For a contract to be legally binding, it must contain four essential elements:

1. An **offer** - a proposal to make a contract.

2. An **acceptance** - an agreement to an offer resulting in a contract.

3. **Consideration** - the bargained-for exchange in a contract.

4. **Contractual capacity** - the legal ability to enter into a contract.

Note: An in-depth review of the these four contract elements is provided in the next chapter

Classification of Contracts

While there is no true definitive collection of contract rules, there is guidance available from three primary resources:

1. Common Law - This body of law is derived from judicial decisions rather than from legal statutes or constitutions.

2. Restatement of Contracts, 2nd ed. - This publication is a project of the American Law Institute to reduce contract law down to a set of black letter rules to inform judges and lawyers about general principles of contract common law. While helpful, the problem with this resource is it has limitations, as it represents law that has not been enacted but is nonetheless considered persuasive authority for lawyers and the courts.

3. Uniform Commercial Code (UCC) - The **Uniform Commercial Code** is a model act that includes provisions concerning certain sales of goods and negotiable instruments.

The classification of contracts may be based on their:

- formation,
- performance, or
- enforceability.

Classification of Contracts - Based on Formation

Express contracts - An **express contract** is one in which the parties express their intentions – either orally or in writing – at the time of the agreement. Contractual agreements to provide funeral services are an express written contract between the funeral establishment and the person with the priority right to control the final disposition of human remains.

In most states, establishments have three options when it comes to having a written contract for funeral services.

1. Including contractual language within the FTC mandatory Statement of Funeral Goods and Services Selected (Statement). This document then serves two purposes: 1) a written express contract to provide goods and services; and 2) fulfillment of the FTC requirement to provide an itemized statement to the consumer at the conclusion of funeral arrangements that enumerates those goods and services.

2. Having a stand-alone, express written contract in addition to the mandatory FTC Statement.

3. Including the information required on the FTC Statement in the express written contract used by the establishment. The FTC Funeral Rule specifically provides for this third option and in reference to the itemized statement has stated:

   The information required on the statement can be included on a contract or any other document that you give to customers at the conclusion of the arrangements discussion.

Statute of Frauds

In most circumstances, an oral contract is legally enforceable; however, there are contracts that must – to be legal and enforceable – be in writing. The **Statute of Frauds** was enacted under English Law in 1677 and stipulated certain contracts had to be in writing to be enforceable.

James Chen, in an article on the Investopedia website, has noted:

> *The statute of frauds was adopted in the U.S. primarily as a common law concept – that is, as unwritten law. However, it has since been formalized by statutes in certain jurisdictions, such as in most states. In a breach of contract case where the statute of frauds applies, the defendant may raise it as a defense.*

Today, most states have adopted the Statute of Frauds to identify those contracts that must be in writing to be enforceable, although the statutes may vary by state. The requirement to have a contract in writing only applies to executory contracts – a contract in which the terms have not been completely executed or fulfilled. It is noteworthy that once a contract is completed (executed), it cannot be canceled after the fact because it was not in writing.

The six categories of contracts that must be in writing to be enforceable under the Statute of Frauds typically include:

1. Promises in consideration of **M**arriage.

2. Executory contracts which cannot be completed within one **Y**ear.

3. Contracts involving real property - **L**and and objects permanently attached to the land.

4. Contracts made by an **E**state fiduciary to pay estate debts using personal funds.

5. **G**uaranty or promising to pay the debts of another.

6. **S**ale of goods when the price is $500.00 or more.

The six categories can be remembered by using the mnemonic **MY LEGS**, which stands for **M**arriage, **Y**ear, **L**and, **E**state, **G**uaranty, and **S**ale.

Promises in consideration of marriage - Mutual promises to marry do not fall under the Statute of Frauds; however, the requirement to have a contract in writing does apply if an agreement to marry is made in consideration of some promise other than a mutual promise to marry.

For example, if Jim agrees to marry Jane only under the condition she turns certain property over to him, the agreement would not be enforceable if it is not in writing. A court would want proof to demonstrate and establish the parties reached such an agreement.

A prenuptial marriage agreement exists when a couple planning to marry agrees to take on rights and obligations that are not implied obligations of the marriage itself. Any such agreements must be in writing to be enforceable.

Executory contracts which cannot be completed within one year - A contract must be in writing if its terms cannot be completed within one year of the date of agreement. I.e., if a contract can be completed in one year or less from the date of the agreement, it does not need to be in writing. The one-year period begins the day *after* the contract is formed.

For example, Smith owns a funeral home and is planning to take a year off from his business to travel to the Orient with his wife. On March 15, Smith *orally* agrees to hire Jones for one year from May 1 to April 30 to operate and manage the funeral home in his absence. Because the oral contract was made on March 15 and the terms of the contract cannot be completely fulfilled until over one year later on April 30, the contract must be in writing to be enforceable. The date when

Jones is scheduled to take over management (May 1) is not significant and plays no role in whether or not the contract must be in writing.

Contracts involving real property - Real property is defined as land and those objects permanently attached to the land. A contract for the sale of real property consists of an offer by the buyer and an acceptance by the seller, and the contract must be in writing to be enforceable.

There is an exception to the written requirement when there has been a partial performance of an oral agreement. The argument would be partial performance proves the existence of a contract, and a court could rule that the partial performance was sufficient enough to demonstrate the contract is enforceable, regardless of the fact that it is not written.

There are situations where the owner of real property may not want to sell the land but only want to sell an interest in the land. This type of contract must also be in writing. Examples might include a contract that extends a right-of-way into and out of land; grants joint use of a driveway; or transfers the rights to mineral deposits on real property.

Contracts made by an estate fiduciary to pay estate debts using personal funds - A **fiduciary** is. When an person dies, an estate administrator will be responsible for settling the estate of the deceased. The administrator is a fiduciary – a person in a relationship of trust and confidence – charged with inventorying the estate assets and paying estates debts (such as a funeral bill). Thereafter, they distribute any remaining real or personal property assets according to the terms of a will or – if there is no last will – pursuant to state law.

Any outstanding debts of a deceased person are paid out of the estate assets, but the estate fiduciary is not personally responsible to pay these debts. However, a fiduciary can agree to pay estate debts from their own personal funds in unusual circumstances. This scenario is in reality a contract for the fiduciary to become a guarantor (person who will pay the debt if the debtor does not). The debtor in this case is the estate.

Guaranty or promising to pay the debts of another - A guaranty is a promise to pay the debts or settle the wrongdoings of another if the debtor does not personally pay the debt or make a settlement. A debt is an obligation to pay money.

A person who pays the debt of another is a guarantor. A guarantor promise to pay is secondary to the debtor who owes the money. Therefore, if the debtor fails to pay the debt, the guarantor will then be responsible for payment. Given this situation, the Statute of Frauds requires any agreement must be in writing to be enforceable

For example, John works as a laborer for the Brown Funeral Home but wants to attend the Jones School of Mortuary Science and become a funeral director so he can make more money. He applied to the Jones School and was admitted but then had to apply to Smith National Bank for a $35,000 loan to pay tuition fees.

The bank told John he does not have enough credit history to obtain the loan by himself, but they would reconsider if he could get someone with a good credit history to co-sign the loan. John's employer, Michael Smith, agrees to co-sign the loan so John can get the money for the tuition.

In the example:

- The *debtor* is John (*the person who owes the money to the bank*).
- The *debt* is the amount of the loan *($35,000)*.
- The *guarantor* is Michael Smith (*the person who will pay the debt if the debtor does not)*.
- Michael (*the guarantor*) has given a *guaranty* (*promise to pay*).
- If John defaults on payments to the bank, Mike (the guarantor) will be legally obligated to pay the debt.

Sale of goods when the price is $500.00 or more - This Statute of Frauds requirement applies to most purchases of goods and is included in the Uniform Commercial Code, a model act that includes provisions concerning certain sales of goods and negotiable instruments. Goods are defined as movable, tangible personal property. When the price for the sale of personal property is $500.00 or more, there must be a written contract for the purchase.

Other written contracts required - In addition to contracts required to be in writing under the Statute of Frauds, there may be similar requirements in state statutes, laws, rules or regulations. For example, documents for the sale of securities, agreements to pay a commission to a real estate broker, or a promise to extend a statute of limitations often must be in writing pursuant to state laws. It is therefore important for funeral service practitioners to familiarize themselves with any federal, state, and local requirements concerning contracts in the jurisdictions where they practice.

To satisfy the Statute of Frauds, a written agreement, memorandum, note, or other record should contain the following information:

- The names of the parties to the agreement.
- The purpose and intent of the agreement.
- The date and place where the contract was made by the parties.
- The signatures of the parties or at least the signature of the party against whom any enforcement is being sought.

Writings may consist of a single document or group of documents, together with all of the pertinent information for the Statute of Frauds to be satisfied. With the enactment of the federal Electronic Signatures in Global and National Commerce Act (E-Sign Act), the signatures need not be physically signed on paper. This law allows contracts bearing electronic signatures to be valid and enforceable.

Parol Evidence Rule

The Parol (rhymes with barrel) Evidence Rule states any spoken or written words that are in conflict with what a written contract states cannot be introduced as evidence in court. If a written contract is complete, the parol evidence rule prevents any oral testimony or any writing based on a claim that the provisions of a contract do not represent their real intention. When faced with a written contract, the courts presume the parties agreed upon all the terms and provisions contained in the contract.

Parol evidence can be admitted if it is found the provisions in a written contract are not complete. In those cases, parol evidence can be admitted to clear up any ambiguities or demonstrate the existence of common trade customs or practices that are considered to be forming a part of the contract. Further, a contract that appears to be complete may have omitted a provision that should have been included. If shown an admission was due to fraud, alteration, typographical errors, or duress – parol evidence may be allowed to clarify the contract terms.

The Cornell Law School Legal Information Institute defines the Parol Evidence Rule as governing:

> *... the extent to which parties to a case may introduce into court evidence of a prior or contemporaneous agreement in order to modify, explain, or supplement the contract at issue. The rule excludes the admission of parol evidence. This means that when the parties to a contract have made and signed a completely integrated written contract, evidence of antecedent negotiations (called 'parol evidence') will not be admissible for the purpose of varying or contradicting what is written into the contract.*

Implied Contracts

These contractual agreements are legally binding on the parties by virtue of the actions, acts, or conduct of at least one of the parties. An **implied contract** is one that is assumed to exist; it does not need to be confirmed in writing or orally. A contract is implied when a party knowingly accepts a benefit from another party in circumstances where the benefit cannot be considered a gift. The party accepting the benefit would then be under a legal obligation to give fair value for the benefit received.

For example, a student is late for class – again – and while driving too fast crashes their car into a ditch. They call a tow truck to come and pull them out. When the towing company pulls the vehicle out of the ditch (a benefit to the student) there is an implied contract they are doing so with the intention of being paid (pulling the vehicle out would not be considered a gift).

The old adage of 'actions speak louder than words' succinctly describes an implied contract.

Quasi-Contracts
This type of contract is created or implied by a court where there is unjust enrichment. Unjust enrichment takes place when an individual receives a material gain at the expense of another person that the law sees as unjust. The function of a **quasi-contract** is to raise an obligation in law where in fact the parties made no promises. An example of a quasi-contract would be when a car accident victim needs immediate medical attention but may not be conscious or is otherwise unable to consent to be treated. Under these circumstances, the law does so on their behalf and creates a legal obligation for the injured party to pay for the medical expenses.

Formal Contract
During the late 19th and early 20th centuries, illiteracy in the United States was very prevalent and widespread. During this time, contracts were often *signed* by affixing a wax impression of a person's insignia or special mark to denote a signature. This practice gave rise to defining a formal contract as one that was 'under seal.'

Today, under seal is – in most applications – known as a legal procedure that provides the means to allow confidential information to be filed with a court without it becoming a matter of public record. Nonetheless, a document may be considered *signed under seal* if the person whose signature is affixed also has an official seal, such as a government representative using the approved seal of the jurisdiction they represent.

Today, a formal contract is defined as a legally enforceable contract that uses a prescribed format and contains standardized conditions and provisions in its text.

Note: Sources that simply define a formal contract as one that is in writing and an informal contract as an oral agreement are *not accurate*.

The official seal for the City of Albuquerque in New Mexico.

E-contract - This type of contract is created electronically and must meet all of the same requirements for a contract under both common law and the UCC. Online sellers making offers should clearly spell out the terms of the offer and have a hypertext link to a page that displays the entire contract in a readable format. In most cases, a buyer can accept by clicking a box stating 'I agree' or 'I accept' an online offer. These agreements may be referred to as a 'click-on agreement.'

The E-Sign Act provides a general rule of validity for electronic records and signatures for certain legal transactions. An e-signature is as valid as a wet ink signature. An e-signature is defined as:

> *... an electronic sound, symbol, or process attached to or logically associated with a record and executed or adopted by a person with the intent to sign the record.*

With the onset of Covid-19, many states made provisions for funeral establishments to use e-contracts when making funeral arrangements, as well as to sign such documents as an authorization to cremate human remains. It is expected many of these provisions will become permanent and common place in the funeral service industry.

Classification of Contracts - Based on Performance
Contracts that exist on the basis of performance include bilateral and unilateral contracts.

Bilateral contract - A **bilateral contract** consists of mutual promises to perform some future acts and is the most common type of contract based on performance. They may be described as an exchange of promises – a promise for a promise. In a bilateral contract, both parties agree to an obligation.

For example, Billy offers to wash and clean Susan's car once a week for four weeks if she promises to do his laundry once a week for the same four weeks. If Susan agrees to those terms, there will have been an exchange of promises – he promises to wash the car and she promises to do the laundry – and a bilateral contract will exist.

Unilateral contract - A **unilateral contract** is a contract formed when an act is performed in consideration for a promise. In a unilateral contract, only the offeror has an obligation. Offerors may use unilateral contracts to make a broad or optional request which is only paid for when certain specifications are met. If an individual or individuals fulfill the specified act, the offeror is required to pay.

For example, the owner of Thornton Funeral Home promises to pay Edward $50.00 whenever he assists him at a funeral. The contract is not effective until Edward actually performs the act to assist the owner with a funeral, and the owner is then obligated to fulfill his promise to pay Edward the $50.00.

Executory versus executed contracts - An **executory contract** is one in which the terms have not been completely executed or fulfilled; and an **executed contract** is one in which the terms have been completely fulfilled.

For example, a local funeral director agrees to work for the Jones Funeral Home for one year at a monthly salary of $2500. This contract remains an executory contract from the time it is made until the twelve months are completed; at which time – if all the terms have been fulfilled – it becomes an executed contract.

Classification of Contracts - Based on Enforceability
Contracts that exist on the basis of enforceability include valid, void, voidable, and unenforceable contracts.

Valid contract - A **valid contract** is one which is legally enforceable and can be enforced by either of the parties by going before a court of law. Valid contracts contain the four essential elements of a contract: an offer, an acceptance, contractual capacity, and consideration.

Void contract - A **void contract** is an agreement which has no legal effect or validity and cannot be enforced by either party. For example, if Jim has a signed a written contract to sell a car to a distant cousin in Alabama for $1000, and it is later determined Jim does not actually own the car or the have any right to sell the car, the contract would be void because Jim did not disclose a material fact to the cousin. Any instance of misrepresentation, fraud, undue influence, or duress voids a contract.

Voidable contract - A **voidable contract** in one which would be an enforceable agreement, but due to circumstances may be set aside by one of the parties. The key here is that a voidable contract is only binding on one of the parties. The other party (to which the contract is not binding) may elect to withdraw from the contract or enforce the contract. For example, a contract that was made at a time when one of the parties was under mental duress or impairment, or not of a legal age to execute a contract, could be voidable by that party.

Unenforceable contract - An **unenforceable contract** is an agreement which is not in a form required by law. While possibly legal, an unenforceable contract has failed to meet some specific requirement of the law and therefore cannot be enforced by either of the parties. For example, an oral contract to purchase real property subject to the Statute of Frauds that requires the contract be in writing would not be enforceable by either party in a court of law.

Chapter 5: Elements of a Contract

Overview

The four essential elements of a contract are an offer, an acceptance, contractual capacity, and consideration. This chapter discusses each of these elements in depth.

Chapter Definitions

Contract - a legally enforceable agreement.

Counteroffer - a change to an original offer that in effect, rejects that offer and becomes a new offer.

Creditor - a person or entity to whom money is owed.

Disaffirmance - election to avoid a voidable contract.

Minor - those persons under legal age; for most states, the standard is under the age of eighteen.

Necessaries - items required for living at a reasonable standard (i.e., food, clothing, and shelter).

Offeree - the party to whom an offer is made.

Offeror - the party who initiates or makes an offer.

Promissory estoppel - An equitable doctrine that prevents the promisor from revoking the promise when the promise justifiability acts in reliance upon the promise to his or her detriment.

Ratification - approving an act which was executed without authority; electing to be bound by a voidable contract.

Rejection - refusal to accept.

Revocation - cancellation of an instrument by the maker or drawer; rescinding an offer.

Statute of limitations - a law that restricts the period of time within which an action may be brought to court.

Uniform Commercial Code (UCC) - model act that includes provisions concerning certain sales of goods and negotiable instruments.

Valid contract - a contract which is legally enforceable.

Void contract - an agreement of no legal effect.

Voidable contract - a contract which would be an enforceable agreement, but due to circumstances may be set aside by one of the parties.

Contract Elements

For a **contract** to be legally binding, it must contain four essential elements:

1. An offer - a proposal to make a contract.

2. An acceptance - an agreement to an offer resulting in a contract.

3. Consideration - the bargained-for exchange in a contract.

4. Contractual capacity - the legal ability to enter into a contract.

An offer and an acceptance are often called mutual assent or a 'meeting of the minds' between the parties. Mutual assent – together with the consideration and contractual capacity elements – meet the requirements for a legally binding agreement.

The Offer

An offer is a proposal to make a contract. The **offeror** is the party who initiates an offer, and the **offeree** is the person to whom an offer is made. When a court is looking at whether or not a contract has been formed, they use an '*objective theory of contracts*' to determine the validity of the agreement. This theory provides for a court to look to the words and conduct of the offeror as they would be understood by a reasonable person. The factors considered might include what the parties said, what was said regarding the language of the contract, and how the average individual could interpret what was said by the offeror. Under this theory, subjective intentions (secret or inner feelings) between the parties are not considered.

For an offer to be valid it must be:

- definite,
- seriously intended, and
- communicated to the offeree.

Offer must be definite - To be definite, the offer should specify all of the terms and conditions in the contract. The terms required to be stated include the identity of the offeree; the subject of the offer; and the price, quantity, and time of performance. Demonstrating these terms are present is important to counter any disagreement between the parties should a dispute arise.

In contrast, the **Uniform Commercial Code** (UCC) modifies the strict common law rule in the sale of goods, whereby an omission of one or more essential terms does not necessarily make an offer invalid as long as the agreement has sufficient information to demonstrate the parties intended to enter into a contractual agreement. For example, an offeror could state the price for goods being sold will be determined by the market price at a future date or by a third party, or may not specify any price at all, in which case the offeree (buyer) must pay a reasonable value for the goods.

Offers must be seriously intended - A valid offer must show the offeror intended to be bound by the offer if accepted. Intent must be an outward expression of the offeror and not by any secret intentions. Offers made in jest, anger, or under severe emotional strain are not binding.

For example, Jim is attempting to use his new $2000 lawnmower to cut his grass, but the machine is not working properly. After several failed attempts, Jim is totally frustrated and yells to his neighbor Bob, "I'll sell you this piece of garbage for $10." Bob yells back, "You've got a deal," and walks over to give Jim $10. Because Jim was angry when he made the offer to sell the lawnmower, it was *not* a valid offer, and he is not obligated to sell the lawnmower to Bob. Nonetheless, there may be times when a person jokingly says something that is not intended to be an offer, but the offeree is not aware there is a lack of intent and accepts. A court would then have to exercise the 'objective theory of contracts' to determine if a **valid contract** was made.

Offer must be communicated to the offeree - An offeror must make the offer directly to the offeree. This may be accomplished in person; by telephone, letter, fax, e-mail, or text message; or any other form of communication. Unless some other provision has been made, when an offer is made to a specific person that individual alone has the power to accept the offer.

Non-Offers or Invitations to Deal

Offers made between named individuals are fairly straightforward; however, the process can get complicated when there is little to no contact between the parties. In business environments, there are times when what may appear to be an offer is actually not an offer at all. They may simply be an invitation to the public to make an offer on certain terms or prices. The most common 'non-offers' are:

- advertisements,
- price lists and quotations, and
- bids and estimates

Advertisements - As seen or heard every day on television, over the radio, in a newspaper or a magazine, or browsing the internet – an advertisement is treated as an invitation to negotiate, not as an offer. Advertisements do not usually include sufficient language and information to express a clear commitment to an offering to be considered for the purposes of a contract. For example, if a shoe store runs an ad in the local newspaper advertising shoes on sale for $15.00 a pair, there is an insufficient amount of information to constitute an offer.

An advertisement can be considered an offer if the language is specific to a particular individual or group of persons. For example, "Come to our store at 10 am this Friday to buy the only outdoor furniture set we have in stock for $400.00 – first come, first served." This statement could be considered an offer, as it is limited to only one person. Offering a reward to apprehend a criminal or return lost property could also be valid contract offers, since the number of offerees who can accept the rewards is limited, making them definite and binding. To avoid any possibility of an advertisement being considered an offer, merchants often attach a conspicuous disclaimer stating the advertisement is an invitation to make an offer to buy something.

Price lists and quotations - These are other methods used to portray an invitation to negotiate or trade. However, the price list of an offeror is not an offer to sell at a particular price; it is an invitation to a potential buyer to offer to buy at that price. In many instances, a seller indicates 'prices are subject to change' on a price list to avoid any uncertainty as to whether a price is an offer or an invitation.

Bids and estimates - A bid is an offer to do work or provide services for a specific price in competition with other offers. An estimate approximates what goods or services will cost. Both bids and estimates are seen as requests for an offer only. They are considered an invitation to negotiate or request a proposal, but ultimately can be accepted or rejected by the entity calling for the bid.

For example, a bid may be made in the setting of an auction when an auctioneer 'invites' members of the audience to make offers, and the audience reciprocates by making offers in the form of a bid. If it is an auction 'with reserve,' the auctioneer is not obligated to accept the seller bid and the seller can withdraw the bid at any time before it is accepted. If an auction is 'without reserve' the auctioneer is not allowed to withdraw the item from sale once a bid is made and must sell to the highest bidder.

Termination of an Offer

An offer can be terminated in any one of seven different ways:

1. Revocation
2. By terms of the offer
3. By lapse of a reasonable time
4. Upon the death or insanity of either party
5. Rejection
6. Counteroffer
7. Intervening illegality

Revocation - With some exceptions, an offeror will usually have the right to withdraw or rescind an offer at any time before acceptance. A **revocation** may be stated either orally or in writing but must be clearly communicated to the offeree. The revocation is effective upon actual communication to the offeree.

By terms of the offer - If the offer contains specific terms indicating how long it remains open, those terms govern whether or not the offer can be terminated. An *option* is a binding promise to hold an offer open if the offeror receives something of value (consideration) in return. When there is an option, an offer cannot be revoked at will and remains open for a specified period of time or until a specific date.

By lapse of a reasonable time - A reasonable timeframe for the purposes of terminating an agreement may be determined by stated terms in the agreement. When not stated, an offer may lapse after reasonable notice has been communicated to the offeree of the intent to terminate the offer. Reasonableness varies depending on the facts and circumstances of each situation. Courts are often called upon to render opinions on the reasonableness of an act and base rulings on whether or not the action taken was reasonable and fair under the circumstances.

Upon death or insanity of either party - There is immediate termination of an offer if either the offeror or offeree dies under any circumstance or becomes incapacitated as a result of mental illness. This occurs even if one party is not aware of the death or insanity of the other party and tenders an acceptance. Both parties must be alive and competent to accept at the time acceptance is communicated. An exception can occur if there is an option contract still viable at the time of a party's death. In those cases, the estate of the deceased would be responsible to carry out the provisions of any contract that includes such an option.

Rejection - A **rejection** is a refusal to accept an offer and thereafter terminates the offer. Once the rejection has been communicated to and received by the offeror, the offer cannot be revived or made into a counteroffer.

Counteroffer - A **counteroffer** is a change to an original offer that in effect rejects the original offer and becomes a new offer. The mirror-image rule – which at common law provided an offer must be accepted without deviation from its terms – may be raised when a counteroffer is made; however, in defining the mirror-image rule, Black's Law Dictionary notes:

> *In modern commercial contexts, the mirror-image rule has been replaced by a UCC provision that allows parties to enforce their agreement despite minor discrepancies between the offer and the acceptance.*

Intervening illegality - If the terms of the offer have been destroyed or become illegal after the offer has been made but before it was accepted, the contract is void.

The Acceptance

An acceptance is the second element of a contract and is defined as an agreement to an offer resulting in a contract. To be valid, the acceptance must be unconditional and communicated to the offeror. When attempting to determine whether or not there has been a valid acceptance of an offer, the following factors may be considered:

- form of acceptance,
- required knowledge of the offer,
- must be communicated to the offeror, and

- must be acceptance by mail, telegram, facsimile, or electronic transmittal.

Form of acceptance - Unless specified in the offer, no particular form of acceptance is required. The offeree's act of acceptance can be made orally, in writing, or by the conduct of the offeree. Common forms of communication – telephone, letter, fax, email, or text – may be used for the purposes of accepting an offer.

Generally speaking, unless the parties agree otherwise, the silence or inaction of an offeree will not be considered an act of acceptance, even if the offeror states it is. An offeree has no obligation to reply even if the offeror makes a provision in the offer that 'failure to reply will amount to acceptance'. Miller states an, "… *offeree should not be burdened by liability to act affirmatively in order to reject an offer* …" especially when the offeree has not given any consideration.

There are times when silence may be viewed as acceptance of an offer. According to Miller, this could occur if the offeree accepts, "… *the benefit of offered services even though the person had the opportunity to reject them and also knew that they were offered with the expectation of compensation.*" For example, this could happen if an offeree had prior dealings with the offeror and there is an established past practice for the offeree to notify the offeror when there is no acceptance, but make no notification when there is acceptance.

Required knowledge of offer - An offeree must first have knowledge of an offer to be able to accept it, and thereafter communicate such acceptance to the offeror.

Must be communicated to the offeror - As the offeror is the party controlling the offer, they also control the mode of communication in which an acceptance must be made. If the mode of communication is specified in the offer, it is the only method by which the offer may be accepted. If no mode of communication is specified in the offer, any of the common forms of communication may be used. The Uniform Commercial Code provides communication of an acceptance may be made, "… *in any manner and by any medium reasonable in the circumstances*."

Acceptance by mail, telegram, facsimile, or electronic transmittal - Unless specified or implied based on facts and circumstances, Ashcroft states, "*The particular manner of acceptance may be accepted in any manner reasonable under the circumstances*." Acceptance occurs based on the agreement of the parties, which may specifically state whether acceptance is effective when it is sent by the offeree or when it is received by the offeror.

When there is no stated method for acceptance, a common law construct called the 'mailbox rule' provides an acceptance is binding when properly addressed, stamped, and dropped into a mailbox or given to a postal employee to mail. The acceptance is still effective even if the offeror never receives the acceptance.

A telegram is effective at the time it is given to the telegraph company to be sent. Regarding a facsimile or fax, the contract is made "… *on the date and at the place where the fax acceptance is sent*," according to Ashcroft.

Electronic transmittals have become an important part of commerce, and the Uniform Electronic Transactions Act provides – in those cases where the offeror and offeree agree to use an electronic transmittal – an email acceptance of an offer becomes effective when sent.

If an offeror authorizes a specific method of acceptance but the offeree uses a different method, the offer can still be accepted; however, it is not deemed to be accepted until it is received by the offeror. As long as the substituted method of service *serves the same purpose as the authorized method*, acceptance can be made.

For example, Fred makes an offer to Sam and authorizes FedEx shipping as the method of acceptance. Sam could not get his acceptance of the offer shipped via FedEx, so he opted to use UPS overnight delivery. The acceptance Sam sent would be valid, as the method he used 'served the same purpose as the authorized method.'

Consideration

Consideration is the third element of a contract and defined as the bargained-for-exchange in a contract, and West's Encyclopedia of American Law describes consideration as:

> *Something of value given by both parties to a contract that induces them to enter into the agreement to exchange mutual performances.*
>
> *Consideration is an essential element for the formation of a contract. It may consist of a promise to perform a desired act or a promise to refrain from doing an act that one is legally entitled to do.*
>
> *In a bilateral contract – an agreement by which both parties exchange mutual promises – each promise is regarded as sufficient consideration for the other.*
>
> *In a unilateral contract – an agreement by which one party makes a promise in exchange for the other's performance – the performance is consideration for the promise, while the promise is the consideration for the performance.*

There are two elements to consideration: 1) legally sufficient value, and 2) bargained-for exchange.

Legally sufficient value - Consideration must be something that has value and is recognized in the law. Miller states value may be viewed as:

- a promise to do something that one has no prior legal duty to do;
- performing some action that one is otherwise not obligated to take; or
- refraining from an action that one has a legal right to do (forbearance).

Example 1: Dan owns a 2010 Subaru with 50,000 miles on it and Ben has offered Dan $5,000 for the car. Dan accepts the offer. This a bi-lateral contract – an agreement by which both parties exchange mutual promises.

Example 2: Jack says to Mike, if you drive my car from New York to Seattle for me, I will pay you $1000. This is a unilateral contract – an agreement by which one party makes a promise (money) in exchange for the other's performance (drive the car to Seattle).

Example 3: Jim, the owner of the Smith Funeral Home in Peekskill is selling his business to Bill; and Bill wants Jim to agree that if he buys the funeral home, Jim will not open a funeral home within 25 miles of Peekskill for at least five years. This is an example of forbearance, where Jim agrees to refrain from opening a funeral home, although he would have a legal right to do so.

Bargained-for exchange - According to Miller, the bargained-for exchange element of consideration requires an "*... item of value must be given or promised by the promisor in return for the promisee's promise, performance or promise of performance.*"

In his book, Scott Burnham recommends going through a brief question and answer session to determine whether or not consideration is present. Using Example 1 above, questions and answers between Dan and Ben concerning the sale of a car might go something like this:

> Dan: Why did I promise you the car?
>
> Ben: So you could get my promise of $5000.
>
> Dan: And why did you promise me the $5000?
>
> Ben: So I could get the car.

Since a promise and a performance were exchanged by the parties to the agreement, the third element of a contract – consideration – was met. Both Dan and Ben each received what the other wanted and had agreed upon.

Adequacy of consideration - Courts recognize parties are free to enter into a contract on mutually agreed upon terms. And generally speaking, a court will not question the adequacy of the consideration in an agreement as long as it is sufficient. Individuals can be a party to a bad agreement, but if anyone could file a legal claim against another party simply because they themselves made a poor decision, courts would be inundated with frivolous lawsuits. Nonetheless, when there is a great disparity in the amount or value of consideration, a court may look closely at the agreement out of concern for any potential fraud, duress, or undue influence.

Consideration and the Uniform Commercial Code (UCC) - Contracts that involve the sale of goods are within the jurisdiction the UCC and – in certain types of contracts – the UCC does not require the consideration element for the contract to be valid. These include:

- a merchant's written firm offer that specifies the contract is irrevocable;
- a written discharge of a claim for an alleged breach of contract; and
- a modification of an existing contract.

The UCC also provides any claim arising out of an alleged breach of contract can be discharged – in whole or part without consideration – by a written document signed by the aggrieved party. These documents are known as a 'general release,' and a general release can be considered valid consideration if that is the intent of the parties, as it would be viewed as a form of forbearance.

<u>Contracts that Lack Consideration</u>
Pre-existing duty - A contract that includes an obligation for a party to perform an act for which they are already bound to perform by law or other agreement would be invalid, as there is no additional sacrifice.

For example, Joe cares about his nephew Bob – a newly licensed driver – and tells him he will give him $1000 is he does not receive a speeding ticket for a year. A year later, after Bob had not received any speeding tickets, he went to see his uncle to collect his $1000. Joe said he was only kidding and just wanted Bob to drive safely.

In this case, Bob could not sue his uncle to recover the $1000 because he had a preexisting duty to comply with vehicle and traffic laws, and there was therefore no valid consideration in the agreement between him and his uncle.

Past consideration - A promise made for an act that has already taken place is unenforceable. A person can bargain for something current or in the future but not for anything that has happened in the past.

For example, Dave was preparing to take his funeral director exam and his friend Harry was helping him study. Dave passed the exam and was so happy he offered to pay Harry $200 for the time he spent helping him study. A month later, Harry called and asked when he was going to get his $200. Dave told him he did not have a job and was not going to pay him the $200.

In this case, Harry could not sue his friend to recover the $200 because the promise was to pay for help studying, a performance that had already been completed *before* the promise was given.

Illusory promises - An illusory promise is an open-ended statement alleging to be an agreement. They are unenforceable because they are not conclusive and speak to something that may or may not happen in the future.

West's Encyclopedia of American Law describes an illusory promise as:

> *A statement that appears to assure a performance and form a contract but, when scrutinized, leaves to the speaker the choice of performance or non-performance, which means that the speaker does not legally bind himself or herself to act.*

For example, the owner of Tom's Funeral Service promises to buy 'such arterial fluid as I may wish to order from the Acme Fluid Co.' The promise is illusory because the owner has not bound himself to any specific terms and is free to buy arterial fluid from anyone else or to not buy any fluid at all from Acme.

Enforceable Promises Without Consideration

Promissory estoppel - **Promissory estoppel** may also be referred to as detrimental reliance. It is an equitable doctrine that prevents a promisor from revoking a promise when the promisee justifiably acts in reliance on that promise to their detriment (disadvantage). Promissory estoppel may be a substitute for consideration.

Ashcroft notes there are four elements to promissory estoppel:

1. A promise is made.
2. The promisor reasonably expects the promise to induce action by the promisee.
3. The promisee does act.
4. Justice requires enforcement of the promise.

For example, Andy Baker – an alumnus of Acme School of Mortuary Science and owner of ten funeral homes – has promised Acme he will give them $2 million for a new clinical embalming wing. Acme erects a plaque announcing the new wing and purchases new embalming tables, instruments, embalming machines, and supplies in preparation for the new facility and otherwise depends on the promise given to them by Mr. Baker.

If Baker reneges on his promise to give the school the funds, Acme – having already spent $350,000 to their own detriment – may rely on the promissory estoppel doctrine to recover at least the amount they already spent and could potentially recover the full $2 million.

Charitable subscriptions - A promise (pledge) to make a gift to a charitable, religious, educational, or scientific organization that depends on voluntary contributions is usually enforceable without consideration. The courts in most states enforce these promises as a matter of public policy, and Ashcroft notes there are two theories on why these charitable subscriptions are binding:

1. Each subscribers promise is supported by the promises of other subscribers.
2. A charitable donation is an offer of a unilateral contract that is accepted by a charity; and the charity is creating liabilities or making expenditures by relying on the promise.

State laws vary on how donations must be pledged, such as whether or not a pledge card must be signed by the person making the pledge for it to be valid.

Promises to pay debts barred by Statute of Limitations - **Statute of limitations** is a law that restricts the period of time within which an action may be brought to court. Each state has a statute of limitations which prevents (bars) a **creditor** from collecting a debt from a debtor after a set period of time. These times vary by state but usually run between three and six years, with six-year statutes the most common.

There are times when a debtor may want to enter into a new agreement to repay a debt, even though the time period for a creditor to file a claim has passed. Since the debtor no longer has a legal duty to pay the debt, the debtors promise cannot serve as consideration. A court may make an exception if the new agreement is in writing and the court recognizes the previous consideration as an element of the new agreement. A new statute of limitations time period would then start.

Pay debts discharged by bankruptcy - A promise to pay a debt that has been discharged (set aside, dismissed) through bankruptcy may be revived under certain circumstances. The debtor must agree to pay the debt and have the approval of the bankruptcy court to do so. A promise of this type is enforceable, even though it is not supported by consideration. The debtor waives the defense of discharge in bankruptcy so the original debt remains in force.

Contractual Capacity

Contractual capacity is the fourth and last element of a contract and the legal ability to enter into a contract. It is the competence or minimum mental capacity a party must possess to enter into a contractual agreement and be bound by the terms of the contract.

A party may not have the contractual capacity required to enter into an agreement due to:

- age;
- incapacitation; or
- physical condition.

Age - A **minor** is a person under legal age; in most states, the standard is under the age of 18. Majority age is the age a state sets for a minor to become an adult and assume legal responsibility for themselves. There are however states that impose certain age-specific legal restrictions on a person who has reached the age of majority, such as setting the minimum age to buy alcohol or tobacco products.

Contracts to which a minor is a party are voidable at the option of the minor; but an adult cannot avoid a contract with a minor merely because the minor would have the right to void it. In most states, a minor cannot void a contract for **necessaries**, defined as items required for living at a reasonable standard (i.e., food, clothing, and shelter).

Legally incapacitated person - A legally incapacitated person is distinguishable based on whether or not a court has found they lack a required mental capacity. If someone is found by a court to be judicially incompetent, any contract they may have entered into at a time when they were incompetent would be a **void contract,** defined as an agreement of no legal effect. That same person during a period of lucidness – when they have the capacity to fully under the consequences of their actions – may enter into a contractual agreement just like anyone else. Any contract made by a legally incapacitated person is voidable at the option of the incapacitated individual.

Physical condition - A person may not have the requisite contractual capacity to enter into an agreement if – at the time they do so – they are mentally and physically impaired due to alcohol or drug intoxication or impairment. To be voidable, Miller states the person must prove, "… *the intoxication was so severe the individual did not comprehend the legal consequences of entering into the contract.*" Intoxication includes both alcohol and/or drug use. Agreements made while in this physical condition are voidable at the discretion of the intoxicated person.

On regaining sobriety – the now formerly intoxicated person – may affirm or disaffirm the contract made while under the influence of alcohol and/or drugs. This action must be taken soon after a return to sobriety, or any opportunity to disaffirm a contract may be lost. A person declared to be a habitual drunkard cannot make a valid contract but can be found liable for the reasonable value of any necessaries provided.

Enforcement When Contractual Capacity an Issue

Disaffirmance - **Disaffirmance** is an election to void a **voidable contract**. To assert disaffirmance, a person must through words or actions demonstrate an intent to not to be bound by a contract to which they are a party. As noted previously, contracts made by a minor or person under the influence of alcohol or drugs are voidable contracts, and those persons have the option of terminating those agreements by disaffirmance. If the person is a minor, they may disaffirm at any time while underage or within a reasonable time after reaching the age of majority.

When a contract is disaffirmed, any goods or services the person received and still have in their possession because of the contract terms must be returned. A minor can recover any property transferred to an adult as consideration for the contract, even though the property may now be in the possession of a third party.

Ratification - **Ratification** is electing to be bound by an otherwise voidable contract. Following ratification, the previously voidable contract would then be legally binding on the parties and could not be disaffirmed. Ratification of a contract can be made orally, in writing, or be implied by one's actions. Ratification of an agreement must be for the entire contract. One part cannot be affirmed and the other part ratified. For minors, the ratification of an otherwise voidable contract must occur within a reasonable time after reaching the age of majority.

Liability for necessaries - Necessaries are defined as items required for living at a reasonable standard. The most common necessaries are food, clothing, and shelter, although medical services and education are becoming more prevalent in court cases, especially those that involve a dispute between spouses. State provisions related to the liability to pay for necessaries vary considerably.

In contract law, liability for necessaries is most often associated with voidable contracts entered into by minors or persons who were under the influence of alcohol or drugs at the time the agreement was made. These individuals have the option of terminating the agreement, but in most states a liability exists for goods or services they received that would be considered necessaries.

Chapter 6: Contract Activities and Actions

Overview
This chapter presents information on various activities and actions that may be associated with a contract. It reviews defenses to enforcement, termination of contracts, remedies for breach of contracts, assignments, delegation, and third party contracts.

Chapter Definitions
Accord and satisfaction - An agreement made and executed in satisfaction of the rights one has from a previous contract.

Assignee - the party to whom an assignment is made.

Assignment - a means whereby one party in a contract conveys rights to another party, who is not a party to the original contract.

Assignor - the party making the assignment.

Breach of contract - failure or refusal to perform contractual obligations.

Compensatory damages - an award paid to the injured party to cover the exact amount of their loss but no more.

Creditor beneficiary - a third party beneficiary owed a debt by a party to a contract.

Crime - an offense which is injurious to society as a whole.

Delegation - transfer of contractual duties to a third party.

Discharge - any method by which a legal duty is extinguished.

Donee beneficiary - a third party beneficiary to whom no legal duty is owed, and performance is a gift.

Duress - removing one's free will and obtaining consent by means of a threat.

Fiduciary - a person in a relationship of trust and confidence.

Fraud - inducing another to contract as a result of an intentionally or recklessly false statement of a material fact.

Injunction - a judicial order or decree forbidding certain conduct.

Liquidated damages - damages stipulated in a contract to be paid in the event of a breach.

Misrepresentation - false statement of a material fact.

Nominal damages - small amount awarded when there is a technical breach but no injury.

Novation - the substitution of a new party for one of the original parties to a contract, such that the prior contract terminates and a new one substitutes for it.

Punitive damages - an award to the plaintiff in order to punish the defendant.

Rescission - to set aside or cancel a contract.

Specific performance - a remedy by which the court requires the breaching party to perform the contract.

Statute of limitations - a law that restricts the period of time within which an action may be brought to court.

Third party beneficiary - person not a party to a contract, but one whom the parties intend to benefit.

Tort - a private or civil wrong against a person or his or her property, other than by breach of contract, for which there may be an action for damages.

Undue influence - improper influence that is asserted by one dominant person over another, without the threat of harm.

Usurious - exceeding the maximum rate of interest which may be charged on loans.

Defenses to Enforcement

When there is a dispute over a breach of contract, the party being sued may raise a defense to the enforcement of the contract. These are often called affirmative defenses, meaning the party being sued and raising the defense will have the burden of proving the defense if the case goes to trial.

These defenses do not argue the basic facts of the contract or that a breach took place, but instead put forth circumstances that render the claim of a breached contract moot because the defense – if proven – terminates the contract as a matter law. Defenses to enforcement include fraud, undue influence, duress, mistake, and illegality.

Fraud - **Fraud** is defined as inducing another into a contract as a result of an intentional or recklessly false statement of a material fact. It is a deception that can be expressed orally, in writing, or by acts or conduct of the offeror. There are three elements to fraud.

1. Intentional or reckless misrepresentation of a material fact.

2. Justifiable reliance by the offeree.

3. Proof of damages.

Fraud may be committed by **misrepresentation**, concealment, or silence when one has a duty to speak. Misrepresentation is defined as stating an untrue fact, and this defense presents itself as the intentional misrepresentation of a material fact. An express misrepresentation means the party making the offer consciously intends to mislead the offeree. The party making the fraudulent statement must know it is false, thereby demonstrating intent. A material fact is one that is important enough to influence another person's decision, and this can take place with spoken words or through the actions of the party.

A justifiable reliance by the offeree must exist to demonstrate they actually relied on the false statements made by the offeror and thereby suffered a loss or injury. The misrepresentation must be an important factor in getting the offeree to enter into the contract. For the offeree (victim) to recover damages in a lawsuit, there must be actual proof submitted to demonstrate **compensatory damages** – an award paid to the injured party to cover the exact amount of their loss but no more.

Ashcroft explains an innocent misrepresentation of a material fact can occur during negotiations of a contract when a party makes a statement believing it to be true, when in actuality it is false. Courts may consider this contract voidable.

Concealment is a fraud when a person takes specific action to conceal a fact that is material to the contract.

Silence when one has a duty to speak is another way to commit fraud. Generally speaking, neither party to a contract has a duty to disclose facts. However, if a seller knows of a serious defect or problem that the buyer cannot reasonably be expected to learn, the seller may have a duty to come forward and disclose such information. Sellers have a duty to disclose latent defects that cannot be readily ascertained. Miller states, "*When the parties to a contract are in a fiduciary relationship* [one of trust, such as partners, physician and patient, lawyer and client] *there is a duty to disclose material facts*." Failure to do so may constitute fraud.

With respect to fraud, statements of opinion – as opposed to facts – cannot be considered fraudulent. This concept is known as puffing – a mere expression of an opinion. For example, if a salesperson for an urn company tells a funeral director an urn is the best you can buy for the money, he is expressing his opinion and this represents puffing.

Undue influence - **Undue influence** is another defense to enforcement. It is defined as an improper influence asserted by one dominant person over another without the threat of harm. This often occurs with a **fiduciary** relationship of trust and confidence. For undue influence to exist, there must be clear and convincing evidence the person was not acting of their own free will. This could make the contract voidable at the option of the wrongly influenced party.

Duress - As another defense, **duress** means removing one's free will and obtaining consent by means of a threat. A threat can be shown by a concern for a person's physical well-being, evidence of emotional pressure, or signs of economic duress. Coercion – the practice of persuading someone to do something by using force or threats – must be shown to pursue duress as a defense to enforcement. This defense most often tends to arise from economic (financial) rather than physical threats. Duress could make a contract voidable at the option of the person under such threat.

Mistake - Mistake as a defense is a belief not in accordance with the facts. In contracts, a mistake can occur by both parties (known as a mutual or bilateral mistake), or by one party (known as a unilateral mistake). A mistake by both parties to a contract concerning a basic assumption of fact on which the contract was based must have a material effect on the transaction. This generally renders a contract defective and voidable by the person injured, and the contract can also be rescinded by either party.

For example: George made a contract to sell his 1920 Ford Model T to Bill. The car was stored in a garage 50 miles from their homes and – unknown to either of them – the garage and car were destroyed in a fire one day prior to them signing the contract. Bill had spent $5,000 to renovate a storage space to keep the car in and sued George for $5,000 in damages. Because the car was destroyed *before* the contract was signed, George can claim mutual mistake as a defense.

A material mistake by one party to a contract (a unilateral mistake) can occur by ignorance, forgetfulness, poor judgment, or carelessness. This type of contract generally does not render contracts voidable. However, if the non-mistaken party knew or should have known about the mistake, the contract is voidable if the mistake has a material effect on the contract, or if the mistake was caused by the fault of the non-mistaken party.

For example, a fluid salesman submits an offer in writing to sell Jamie a box of arterial fluid for $100. Jamie mails a letter of acceptance, but on receipt of the acceptance the salesman discovers he typed $100 instead of $200 as he had intended. The salesman refused to send the arterial fluid and Jamie sued. Because the mistake by the salesman was due to his carelessness, it had no effect on the contract. Jamie could most likely enforce the contract for $100.

Illegality - Contracts must be for a lawful purpose and executed in a lawful manner. When this does not occur, the contract is void. If the act in question is legal but the manner in performing the act is not the contract is void. If one of the parties is not equally as guilty as the other, the courts may be more lenient on the party less at fault. There are times when a contract may include illegal clauses that cannot be enforced, but the remainder of the contract would be enforceable.

Illegal contracts include agreements to commit crimes or torts. A **crime** is an offense which is injurious to society as a whole, such as murder, kidnapping, burglary, larceny, and the sale of illegal drugs. A **tort** is defined as a private or civil wrong against a person or his or her own property – other than by breach of contract – for which there may be an action for damages. Torts include assault and battery, slander, libel, fraud, and infliction of emotional distress. Crimes and torts for the purposes of a contact are illegal, thereby rendering the contract void.

Illegal contracts also include agreements that are prohibited by law or are contrary to public policy. States vary on how they view what constitutes a violation of public policy, but Black's Law Dictionary defines public policy as meaning the, "*... collective rules, principles, or approaches to problems that affect the commonwealth or promote the general good.*"

Illegal contracts include these six specific types of agreements:

1. Usurious agreements - **Usury** is defined as exceeding the maximum rate of interest which may be charged on loans. Interest is a fee paid by a borrower to a lender for the use of money, and almost every state has a statute that sets the maximum rate of interest that can be legally charged. These set rates are specific to loan agreements and when exceeded are illegal.

See the chapter titled, *Consumer Protections - Part 2*, for a full review of usury laws.

2. Agreements in restraint of trade - The United States is a market-oriented economy and competition in the free market encourages lower prices, improved products, and better service. However, monopolies can occur when one or more people or firms control the market in a specific area or a certain product. Monopolies are illegal, and there are several federal and state anti-trust laws that regulate trade business agreements, such as the Sherman Antitrust Act that prohibits certain agreements that tend to unreasonably inhibit competition, fix prices, allocate territories, or limit production. The watchword when dealing with restraint of trade is 'competition,' and any agreements that unreasonably restrain trade or competition would be void.

See the chapter titled, *Consumer Protections - Part 2*, for a full review on the Sherman Antitrust Act and other major antitrust laws.

3. Agreements to fix prices - As noted previously, the Sherman Antitrust act is applicable in these circumstances, as they affect *interstate* commerce. Most states have similar laws applicable to *intrastate* commerce, and any agreements written for the purposes of fixing prices would be void.

4. Agreements injurious to public service - Advocacy before a government or other public body is all for the public good, and a robust exchange with these public bodies regarding the passage or defeat of a particular piece of legislation is what is meant to occur in good government. As such, any agreement to use improper influences or tactics, such as bribery, that would be injurious to public service would be void. Other examples of agreements injurious to public service include the use of an improper influence to obtain a pardon or parole, or to secure a public contract. In these cases, the agreements would be void.

5. Agreements to obstruct justice - Examples of agreements to obstruct justice would include agreements to conceal a crime, to not prosecute a crime, to give false testimony or suppress evidence, or to bribe a juror or court official. Any agreement to obstruct justice would be void.

6. Agreements by unlicensed individuals - All states require certain professionals to be licensed by the government before they may perform specified services for the public. Physicians, lawyers, funeral directors, and certified public accountants are all examples of those who must have licenses to practice.

Whether an agreement with an unlicensed person is legal and enforceable depends on the purpose of the licensing statute. If the statutes' purpose is to protect the public from unauthorized individuals, then a contract with any such unlicensed person is generally illegal and unenforceable. The unlicensed individual may also face criminal charges. If the licensing law is meant to raise government revenues, the contract with the unlicensed individual may be enforced, although the unlicensed individual may still face fines and/or imprisonment for violating the law.

Termination of Contracts

A **discharge** is any method by which a legal duty is extinguished. Nevertheless, a discharge can occur only when the parties either collectively or individually have completed their part of the contract. A discharge successfully terminates a contractual relationship between the parties. The discharge (or termination) can be accomplished by:

Performance	Statute of limitations
Agreement	Alteration of a written contract
Bankruptcy	Impossibility of enforcement

Discharge by performance - Ashcroft details five factors to determine whether performance has occurred:

1. Time of performance - A contract that states when performance occurs must be followed precisely. If time is an issue, the contract should state: 'time is of the essence.' If time is not an issue, then performance would be complete within a reasonable time.

2. Tender of performance - An offer to perform a satisfactory obligation under the contract is said to be a tender of performance. Tender is an unconditional offer to perform by a person who is ready, willing, and able to do so. Accordingly, a seller who has made goods available to the buyer has tendered performance and may demand payment pursuant to the terms of the contract.

3. Tender of payment - An offer to pay money for a debt or claim by a buyer and actual payment that will satisfy the seller is called tender of payment. This means the complete amount due and payable under the contract – including interest and costs – must be paid. A buyer who offers to pay for goods and has paid by legal tender can then demand delivery of the goods. Legal tender is in the form of any U.S. money.

4. Complete and satisfactory - A contract is concluded when the parties have completely fulfilled their duties under the agreement. If the party's performance is perfected (achieved), the contract is said to be discharged.

5. Substantial performance - This occurs when a party in good faith has performed all of the promised terms and conditions of a contract, with the possible exception of minor details that do not materially affect the intent of the agreement. Ashcroft notes that performance of the contract must be so nearly complete that it would be a great injustice

to deny the person who is performing the contract payment. Any part of a contract that is not performed can be compensated by awarding damages.

Discharge by performance may also be triggered by a material breach of the contract. A **breach of contract** occurs when there is a failure or refusal to perform contractual obligations. If there has been an inexcusable failure to substantially perform the terms of a contract, the injured party can treat the contract as concluded and be relieved of the duty to perform. The injured party may also sue for monetary damages.

An anticipatory breach is a breach of contract that happens before the time of performance has occurred. The breaching party may simply say, 'I am not going to perform any of the conditions to the contract.' The injured party may then declare the contract terminated and now – having been released from the obligations under the contract – sue for damages. The injured party does not have to wait to sue until the time to perform has passed.

Discharge by agreement - The parties to a contract may have a mutual agreement to terminate or cancel an agreement. In these cases, the contract is simply discharged.

Another means to discharge by agreement is **novation** – the substitution of a new party for one of the original parties to a contract, such that the prior contract terminates and a new one substitutes for it. The terms of the contract remain the same but with different parties. An intent to enter into a novation must be demonstrated, but it does not need to be in writing as it can be implied from the circumstances.

Discharge by agreement may also take place through **accord and satisfaction** – an agreement made and executed in satisfaction of the rights one has from a previous contract. In essence, this is a breach of contract, except the parties make a new contract. The 'accord' is an agreement by one party to accept from the other party performance different from the agreement in the original contract. The 'satisfaction' is the actual performance of the accord. Both accord and satisfaction must occur before the contract is discharged.

For example, Joe borrowed $400 from Sam to help pay his college tuition. When the debt became due, Joe could not come up with the $400. Sam agreed to accept Joe's stereo set in place of the $400 (the accord). The original agreement would then only be discharged when Sam receives and accepts the stereo set (the satisfaction).

Discharge by bankruptcy - Bankruptcy is a legal proceeding to declare a debtor is bankrupt. The court supervises the inventorying and collection of debtor assets and then apportions the distribution of those assets to the creditors owned money. The debtor receives a discharge by bankruptcy that releases them from any further personal liability for any current debts or contracts they have with the creditors.

Discharge by Statute of Limitations - **Statute of limitations** is a law restricting the time period when an action may be brought to court. The time periods vary from state to state. After the time to file a lawsuit has passed, the injured party cannot sue to enforce the rights under the contract. However, it may be possible to revive a debt barred from the statute of limitations depending on the state where the contract was formed. This can occur where there is a written acknowledgement or promise to pay the debt. Some states allow revival by part payment of the debt. Finally, there can be revival by a payment of interest on the debt. If any of these situations occur, the statute of limitations begins to run again from the time of revival.

Discharge by alteration of a written contract - If one of the parties to a contract intentionally and without permission of the other party alters the contract, the injured party may be discharged. The change must be a material alteration, such as a quantity or price term. The individual altering the contract could be held to the original terms or the terms as altered.

Discharge by impossibility of enforcement - Once a contract is made, performance may become impossible. Impossibility is an unforeseen event that prevents a party from performing a contract as promised.

The following situations demonstrate impossibility, thus leading to the discharge of a contract.

> Destruction of the subject matter - If subject matter essential to the performance of a contract is destroyed through no fault of the parties, the contract is discharged. However, it may not be discharged if an event occurs that can be anticipated. Any payment made in advance should be returned when the contract is discharged.
>
> Intervening illegality - Ashcroft states that if an act was legal at the time the contract was made but becomes illegal at a later time, the contract is discharged. However, if one of the parties deliberately causes the contract to become illegal, that party can be held liable.
>
> Death or disabling illness - A contract may be considered impossible to perform if it can be demonstrated the contract requires special skill or talent possessed by a deceased or incapacitated person. Ashcroft notes, "*If the performance is too personal to be delegated, the death or disability of the party bound to perform will discharge the contract.*"

Remedies for Breach of Contract

Remedies for breach of contract include damages, recission, specific performance, and injunction.

Damages - For the failure or refusal to perform contractual obligations, the law allows the injured party to sue for monetary damages. Generally speaking, the purpose of monetary damages in a contract situation is to return the injured party to the same position they were in before the contract was formed.

There are four types of damages:

1. Nominal - **Nominal damages** are a small amount awarded when there is a technical breach but no injury. They are a token award to symbolize vindication of the wrong done to the plaintiff. Often a nominal award is $1.00.

2. Compensatory - Compensatory damages are an award paid to an injured party to cover the exact amount of their loss but no more. It is important to note the injured party has a duty

to mitigate (lessen) any damages, meaning they must attempt to minimize damages to prevent them from increasing, thereby maintaining the principle of compensatory damages.

3. Punitive - **Punitive damages** are an award paid to the plaintiff in order to punish the defendant. They are not meant to compensate the plaintiff and are more prevalent in tort actions than contract disputes.

4. Liquidated - **Liquidated damages** are those damages stipulated in a contract to be paid in the event of a breach. The parties must intend to agree to liquidated damages before any breach could occur. They must be reasonable and should only be provided for when actual damages are difficult or impossible to prove.

Consequential damages may be part of an award for a breach of contract because the damages were or should have been foreseeable by the breaching party. For example, a contractor could breach a contract by not completing renovations to a business facility before a specified deadline in the agreement. In this case, a court may award consequential damages to the business to compensate them for the loss of revenue resulting from the business remaining closed.

Rescission - A **rescission** as a remedy for breach of contract sets aside or cancels a contract. The parties are restored to the original positions they occupied prior to entering into a contract. This remedy tends to occur when the breaching party induced the injured party to enter a contract by fraud, duress, or undue influence.

Specific performance - **Specific performance** is a contract remedy by which a court requires the breaching party to perform the obligations under the contract. This remedy is limited in scope to cases in which the subject matter is rare or unique and an identical item cannot be purchased elsewhere. For example, the sale of land or an interest in real estate is considered unique, and monetary damages cannot fully compensate the buyer. Therefore, a sale contract may be subject to a suit seeking specific performance (completion of the sale). Specific performance can also be court-ordered with contracts for the sale of rare paintings, books, antiques, or heirlooms.

As a general rule, specific performance for a personal services contract will not be ordered, as this would run afoul of the 13th Amendment to the U.S. Constitution with respect to involuntary servitude. The party that breaches the contract could be sued for other types of damages.

Injunction - An **injunction** is a judicial order or decree forbidding certain conduct. An injunction may be the only option available when damages, recission, and specific performance remedies will not adequately compensate for a breach of contract.

<u>Assignments</u>
When two parties enter into a contract there are certain rights and responsibilities that are accorded each party. Common law and the Uniform Commercial Code recognize the parties to a contract may want to transfer their rights. These transfers are known as an **assignment** – a means whereby one party conveys rights to another person who is not a party to the original contract. The parties to an assignment are the **assignor** (party making the assignment) and the **assignee** (party to whom the assignment is made).

Assignments are an important mechanism to transfer rights contained in a contract, especially within the business community. The rights for the payment of money, such as wages, account receivables or royalties; and the rights to the delivery of goods are the most common rights that may be unconditionally assigned without the permission of the other party to the contract.

For example, a banking institution agrees to give a consumer a loan in the form of a mortgage to purchase a home. Thereafter, the bank (as an assignor) assigns their rights under the mortgage to a different lending institution (an assignee). By means of the assignment (transfer of rights), the second institution is then entitled to receive the mortgage payments and service the loan. When unconditional rights under a contract are assigned to another, the assignor no longer has any contract rights and the assignee assumes the right to demand performance (mortgage payments) from the other party to the contract (the home buyer).

Form of notice - Whether or not an assignment must be in writing varies by state, but assignments in writing are preferred by most businesses, especially those offering financial services. In most states, if a contract is in writing any assignment of the rights must also be in writing.

Notice - As a general rule, after an assignment is in effect there is no requirement to give notice to the other party; however, it is a common practice for the assignee to notify all other parties of the assignment. Banks routinely sell mortgages to other financial institutions, and those institutions notify the mortgagees of the rights transfer.

Restrictions - States or municipalities may have restrictions on assignments, such as restricting public works employees from assigning more than a specified maximum percentage of their wages, or the assignment of future earnings from the armed forces.

Delegation

Similar to an assignment (transfer of rights), the parties to a contract may want to transfer their 'duties and obligations' to a third party. This concept is known as **delegation**, and the parties to a delegation are the delegator (party transferring duties to another) and the delegatee (party to whom the duties are transferred).

No special form is needed to create a valid delegation, as the delegator need only express an intention to do so. The delegator remains fully liable under the contract and the other parties to the contract can sue both the delegator and the delegatee for any failure of performance.

Any duty or obligation in a contract may be delegated to a third party, with the exceptions of:

- duties that are personal in nature;
- when performance by a third party will vary materially from that expected by the other party to the contract; and
- when the contract specifically prohibits delegation.

A personal service contract is one in which the terms of the contract require unique skills and/or talent. A contract for personal services cannot be assigned or delegated. Further, an employee cannot be required to work for a new employer without the consent of the employee.

Third Party Beneficiary Contracts

A **third party beneficiary** is not a party to a contract, but one whom the parties intend to benefit. As an intended beneficiary, the third party is in a position to sue the contract offeror if there is a breach of contract.

An intended beneficiary can only enforce the contract once the rights have vested. Vesting occurs when the rights of the third-party beneficiary have taken place and cannot be taken away by the original parties to the contract. Miller states the rights vest for a third-party beneficiary when the they expressly consent to the agreement by acknowledging the contract formed for their benefit; when the third-party materially alters their position in detrimental reliance on the contract; and when the conditions for vesting are satisfied.

The two types of *intended* beneficiaries are a creditor beneficiary and a donee beneficiary.

Creditor beneficiary - A **creditor beneficiary** is a person to whom the promise of a contract owes an obligation or duty which will be discharged to the extent that the promisor performs the promise. For example, if Ben makes a contract to pay a debt Dan owes to Ed, Ed would be the creditor beneficiary of the contract between Ben and Dan.

Donee beneficiary - A **donee beneficiary** is a third-party beneficiary to whom no legal duty is owed and performance is a gift. Once the gift is established, the donee beneficiary can sue the promisor directly to enforce the promise. The most common doner beneficiary contract is a life insurance contract.

A person who *unintentionally* benefits from the performance of a contract and has no rights in the contract is an incidental beneficiary. Ashcroft offers an example where property owners living on a street being paved by a city contractor will receive a benefit from the performance of the contract. However, the property owners are considered incidental beneficiaries and cannot sue the city contractor, as the paving is considered to be furthering the public interest and not to benefit the individual property owners.

Covenants Not to Compete

Black's Law Dictionary defines 'covenant not to compete' as:

> *A promise – usually in a sale-of-business, partnership or employment contract – not to engage in the same type of business for a stated time in the same market as the buyer, partner or employer."*

These covenants are legal and enforceable if the territory and time restrictions are reasonable enough to protect the interests of the buyer. Covenants not to compete are normally interpreted by the courts using the rule of reason, meaning the courts review any covenant in terms of time, geography and what the individual can or cannot do.

Purchase contracts - A purchase contract for a funeral establishment business may have a non-compete clause to protect the interests of the buyer. The clause may restrict the former owner from owning or operating another funeral establishment for a set period of time or within a specified geographic location. It may also restrict the scope of activity of the former owner, such as prohibiting them from seeking future employment as a funeral director; appearing in advertisements for competitor funeral establishments; or recommending preneed customers transfer accounts to a different funeral establishment.

Employment contracts - Employment contracts are designed to protect the interests of a funeral establishment owner from the activities of their employees, both while employed and thereafter, should they be terminated or choose to resign or retire.

Employment contracts may include any of the following:

- covenants not to compete for a specified period of time or within a defined geographical location upon separation from the workplace;

- non-disclosure agreements to protect the confidentiality of customer lists, preneed accounts, and internal workplace operations;

- non-disclosure agreements to prevent the release of any valuable information (trade secrets) that provide the funeral establishment with an advantage over competitors; and

- restrictions on employment outside the workplace, such as working part-time for another funeral establishment; limiting the number of additional outside work hours; or restrictions on the locations or scope of any outside work.

Chapter 7: Uniform Commercial Code Article 2

Overview
The Uniform Commercial Code (UCC) is a group of laws that deal with commercial (business) transactions in the United States. In this chapter, the basic elements of the UCC are discussed as a continuance of the review on contracts in the three previous chapters.

Chapter Definitions
Bill of sale - a document that conveys or evidences title to tangible personal property.

Contract to sell - a contract to sell goods at a future time.

Existing goods - goods which are, at the time of the contract, in existence and owned by the seller.

Future goods - goods not in existence or not yet owned by the seller at the time the contract was created.

Goods - movable tangible personal property.

Identified goods - the goods specified by the buyer and seller.

Intangible personal property - personal property that lacks a physical presence.

Merchant - a person who deals in goods of the kind, or otherwise by occupation purports to have knowledge or skill peculiar to the practices or goods involved in the transaction.

Personal property - all property which is not real property.

Price - the consideration stipulated by contract, generally expressed in money.

Promissory estoppel - an equitable doctrine that prevents the promisor from revoking the promise when the promisee justifiably acts in reliance upon the promise to his or her detriment.

Real property - land and those objects permanently attached to land.

Sale - the transfer of title to goods from the seller to the buyer for consideration.

Service contract - a contract whose subject matter predominantly involves services.

Title - ownership; evidence of ownership of property.

Uniform Commercial Code (UCC) - model act that includes provisions concerning certain sales of goods and negotiable instruments.

Uniform Commercial Code (UCC)
The **Uniform Commercial Code** is recognized as the most important statute in business law, with provisions that regulate certain sales of goods. UCC Article 2 – titled Sales – has been adopted by every state except Louisiana. Article 2 applies to tangible **personal property** classified as goods, such as cars, computers, caskets, urns, and burial vaults. To be classified as **goods**, the item must be tangible and moveable.

Article 2 does *not* apply to:

- **real property**, defined as land and those objects permanently attached to land,

- **intangible personal property**, defined as personal property that lacks a physical presence, such as corporate stocks, checks, and copyrights, or

- **service contracts**, defined as a contract whose subject matter primarily involves services.

Contracts for Goods and Services
There are times – such as in the funeral service industry – when a contract includes both goods and services. In these situations, the courts use a predominant-factor test to determine whether the contract is primarily for the sale of goods or primarily for providing services. If the predominant factor is the sale of *goods* – with the providing of services considered to be incidental – the contract provisions would be governed by the UCC. If the predominant factor is providing *services* – with the sale of goods considered to be incidental – the contract is viewed as a service contract and the UCC would not apply. Service contracts are governed by common law.

For example: In the funeral service industry, a contract for goods and services for a funeral would be considered a service contract (governed by common law), even if the funeral director also sold the family goods, such as a casket or alternative container. The reason is because the predominant factor is providing services in planning and carrying out the funeral; while the sale of a casket or alternative container would be considered incidental.

For another example, a funeral establishment provides direct cremation services to a family. Several months later they return to purchase an urn. While the predominate factor for the direct cremation would have been for services and governed by common law, for this subsequent transaction the predominant factor is the sale of a tangible goods item – the urn – so the sale would be governed by the UCC.

Uniform Commercial Code vs. Common Law
As has been explained, the UCC governs contracts for goods and common law governs contracts for services. What follows next is a review of the major differences between UCC contracts for goods and common law contracts for services.

Offer - Under common law, when a definite offer is met with an unqualified acceptance, a binding contract is formed. The offer must be *definite* enough for the parties to know its essential terms upon acceptance and can be revoked at any time prior to acceptance. There is an exception where the offeree pays consideration for the offeror's irrevocable promise to keep the offer open for a stated period of time, called an option contract.

Under the UCC, a sales contract does not fail for *indefiniteness* even if one or more terms are left open, as long as the parties intended to make a contract and there is a reasonably certain basis for a court to grant an appropriate remedy. The key indicator is the quantity of goods *must* be expressly stated in the contract. If the parties have not agreed upon a price, the courts can determine reasonable price at the time of delivery. If the price is set out by either the buyer or seller, this is done in good faith, defined by the UCC as, "*honesty in fact and observance of reasonable commercial standards of fair dealing*" in the trade.

As opposed to the common law *option contract*, the UCC provides for a 'merchants firm offer,' where the merchant (offeror) gives assurances in a signed writing that the offer will remain open without consideration for a stated period of time or – if no definite period is stated – for a reasonable time but no longer than three months.

Acceptance - Under common law, acceptance can be communicated by the offeree by any authorized mode of communication and is effective on dispatch (transmission), which means the prompt conveyance of the acceptance. If the mode of acceptance is not specified, acceptance can be made by any acceptable means.

An acceptance can be made only by the offeree, and it must be unequivocal under the mirror image rule. If any terms of the contract are added or changed to the acceptance, it is considered a counteroffer and – unless accepted by the offeror – there is no contract.

Under the UCC, acceptance may be made by any reasonable means of communication and is effective on dispatch. However, with a unilateral contract the offeror requires notification of acceptance within a reasonable time by beginning performance, otherwise the offeror can treat the offer as having lapsed before acceptance.

A '*battle of the forms*' dispute may present itself when two businesses or entities are negotiating the terms of the contract and each party wants to contract on the basis of their own terms. However, if the offeree response indicates a definite acceptance of the offer, a contract is formed even if the acceptance includes additional or different terms from those in the offer, unless the seller indicates otherwise.

This may be complicated further depending on whether the parties are merchants or non-merchants. A **merchant** is a person who deals in goods of the kind, or otherwise by occupation purports to have knowledge or skill peculiar to the practices or goods involved in the transaction. 'Goods of a kind' are goods which fall within a group or range of goods produced by a particular industry or industry sector.

When both parties are merchant's, the additional terms automatically become a part of the contract unless:

- the original offer expressly limited acceptance to its terms;

- the new or changed terms materially alter the contract; or
- the offeror objects to the new or changed terms within a reasonable time.

When one or both of the parties is a non-merchant, the contract is formed according to the original offer submitted by the offeror without the additional terms of acceptance.

Consideration - Under common law, consideration is something of a legally sufficient value given in exchange for a promise. There must be a bargained-for-exchange. An option contract requires either consideration or **promissory estoppel**. Promissory estoppel is an equitable doctrine that prevents the promisor from revoking the promise when the promisee justifiably acts in reliance upon the promise to his or her detriment.

Under the UCC, consideration is still a prerequisite to the formation of a valid sales contract. A firm offer from a merchant is irrevocable without consideration, and the UCC does not require new consideration for the modification of a contract.

Statute of Frauds - Under the UCC, the Statute of Frauds applies to contracts for a sale of goods having a price of $500 or more. When it comes to a writing, the Statute requires an assurance that a transaction has occurred, and the quantity of goods *must* be stated. Any other terms may be demonstrated by parol evidence, and the writing must be signed by the party who would attempt to use the Statute as a defense. The UCC allows oral evidence to explain or supplement the written contract by showing a prior course of dealing, usage of the trade, or course of performance. This can occur even if a court finds the writing complete and free from ambiguity.

Note: See the chapter titled, *Classification of Contracts*, for an explanation of parol evidence and a review of the Statute of Frauds under common law.

Terminology Specific to Sales Contracts

Sale - the transfer of title to goods from the seller to the buyer for consideration (price). Ownership changes from the seller to the buyer at the moment the bargain is made regardless of who is in possession of the goods.

For example, the ABC Fluid Company sells two boxes of arterial fluid to the Acme Funeral Home for $200. This is a sale and the buyer has immediate ownership.

Contract to sell - a contract to sell goods at a future time. The buyer does not have the right to possess the goods unless expressly provided for in the contract.

For example, the ABC Fluid Company makes a contract with the Acme Funeral Home to specifically manufacture a cavity fluid for $200. This agreement is a contract to sell, as the cavity fluid to be manufactured by ABC will occur in the future. Title passes to the Acme Funeral Home once the fluid has been manufactured at a later date.

Price - the consideration stipulated by contract, generally expressed in money; however, it can also be expressed by goods or services. Usually a sales contract will have the price stated. If the sales contract does not state the price, it will be determined by the reasonable price for the same goods in the market.

For example, Acme Funeral Home makes a definite agreement with ABC Funeral Supply to purchase five new urns, but the agreement fails to state a price. In this case, a contract has been formed, and the Acme Funeral Home must pay a reasonable price based on the market.

Existing goods - goods which are, at the time of the contract, in existence and owned by the seller.

Future goods - goods not in existence or not yet owned by the seller at the time the contract was created.

Identified goods - the goods specified by the buyer and seller.

Acceptance of Goods by Buyer

The acceptance of goods by the buyer is required for the passage of **title** and occurs when the buyer signifies the intent to retain the goods. Title is defined as ownership, which includes evidence of ownership of property. A **bill of sale** is a document that conveys or shows title to tangible property and may be used to demonstrate title (ownership). While a bill of sale is not necessary to pass title to goods, it may help a buyer prove ownership. Unless unambiguously stated in the language of the contract, an offer to make a contract must be construed as inviting acceptance of the goods in any manner and by any medium reasonable under the circumstances.

Under the UCC, a buyer is permitted to reject goods shipped or delivered to it from a seller if the seller's tender of the goods is in some way not perfect. Known as the 'perfect tender rule,' a seller is obligated to tender goods that exactly match the terms of the contract. This rule existed under common law, and the UCC retained the doctrine by stating that if the goods or the tender of delivery fail in any respect to conform to the terms of the contract, the buyer has the right to either accept the goods, reject the entire shipment, or accept part and reject part.

However, if the seller tenders non-conforming goods before the time of performance has passed – and the buyer rejects those goods – the seller may cure (correct, repair, or replace) the non-conforming goods. If the seller has reasonable grounds to believe the buyer would accept the tendered goods on the buyer's rejection, the seller has a reasonable time to substitute conforming goods without being held liable. If performance becomes commercially impracticable owing to unforeseen circumstances at the time of agreement, the perfect tender rule is no longer in effect.

A buyer can accept goods by words or conduct showing approval by:

- indicating that the goods are conforming;
- indicating that, although the goods are non-conforming, the buyer will accept them;
- by failing to make a valid rejection within a reasonable time; or

- acting in a way inconsistent with the seller's continued ownership, such as by selling the goods.

Once the buyer accepts the goods, payment is due at the contract rate, and a buyer cannot thereafter reject the goods as non-conforming. A buyer may be able to sue for damages based on lateness or non-conformity.

Revocation of Prior Acceptance

A revocation can occur after acceptance when a buyer discovers there has been a breach of the sales contract that *substantially impairs* the value of the goods to the buyer. The buyer must give notice to the seller of the revocation within a reasonable period of time after the buyer should have discovered the defect, but the buyer must explain why they accepted non-conforming goods. There is no definitive legal definition of substantial impairment, and a court may look at whether any alleged defects are easily repaired. If they cannot be easily repaired – or there are so many defects they have a cumulative effect on the goods – a court may find substantial impairment.

The buyer's duties upon revocation are to store, return, or resell the goods. On a rightful revocation of acceptance, the buyer is entitled to all of the purchase price paid, plus consequential damages not preventable by cover. The UCC provides, "*the buyer may 'cover' – by making in good faith and without unreasonable delay – any reasonable purchase of or contract to purchase goods in substitution for those due from the seller*."

Rejection of Goods

If goods purchased do not conform to the terms of the contract, the buyer is entitled to reject them. The buyer must notify the seller of the rejection within a reasonable time after receiving the goods, but the buyer does not have to specify the particular defects to the seller.

The buyer's duties upon rejection are to store the goods with reasonable care for a reasonable time pending the seller's removal, and follow the seller's reasonable instructions to resell the goods if the buyer is a merchant still in possession of the goods. If the seller gives no instructions within a reasonable time, the buyer may:

- store the goods for the seller;
- reship the goods to the seller; or
- resell them for the seller.

There is no duty for the buyer to pay. The goods remain the property of the seller, and the risk of loss also remains with the seller.

Chapter 8: Sales and Warranties

Overview
This chapter focuses on the rules that govern who bears the risk of loss for the shipment of goods. It includes a review of the various types of warranties available and concludes with the requirements to disclaim warranties and thereby avoid liability exposures.

Chapter Definitions
Bill of lading - the contract existing between the consignor and the carrier.

Bill of sale - a document that conveys or evidences title to tangible property.

Common carrier - any carrier required by law to convey passengers or freight without refusal if the approved fare or charge is paid (airline, train, etc.).

Consignee - One who receives goods shipped by common carrier.

Consignor - One who ships good by common carrier.

Creditor - a person or entity to whom money is owed.

Express warranty - the actual and definite statement of a seller, either verbally or in writing, at the time of sale.

Implied warranties - warranties imposed by law, arising automatically because the sale has been made.

Merchant - a person who deals in goods of the kind or otherwise by occupation purports to have knowledge or skill peculiar to the practices or goods involved in the transaction.

Private carrier - those who transport only in particular instances and only for those they chose to contract with (e.g., funeral establishment vehicles and livery).

Service contract - a contract whose subject matter predominantly involves services.

Title - ownership; evidence of ownership of property.

Uniform Commercial Code (UCC) - model act that includes provisions concerning certain sales of goods and negotiable instruments.

Warranties - guarantees made by a seller that an article, good, or service will conform to a certain standard or will operate in a certain manner.

Transfer of Goods and Title
Having entered into a sales contract and identified the goods to be sold, the next step in a sale is for the seller to provide for the delivery of the goods and transfer of **title** (ownership). Goods may

be transported for delivery by a private carrier or a common carrier.

A **common carrier** is any carrier required by law to convey passengers or freight without refusal if the approved fare or charge is paid (airline, train, etc.). **Private carriers** are those who transport only in particular instances and only for those they chose to contract with (e.g., funeral establishment vehicles and livery).

The entity that ships goods by common carrier is the **consignor**, while the entity that receives those goods being shipped by common carrier is the **consignee**. The contract that exists between the consignor (seller) and the carrier is called a **bill of lading**.

West's Encyclopedia of American Law describes a bill of lading as:

> *A document signed by a carrier (a transporter of goods) or the carrier's representative and issued to a consignor (the shipper of goods) that evidences the receipt of goods for shipment to a specific designation and person.*

The seller of goods provides the buyer with a **bill of sale** that conveys or evidences title to tangible property.

West's Encyclopedia of American Law describes a bill of sale as:

> *In the law of contracts, a written agreement ... by which one person transfers to another a right to, or interest in, personal property and goods; a legal instrument that conveys title in property from seller to purchaser.*

<u>Risk of Loss</u>

A contract may require for goods to be sold free on board (FOB) to a designated point. This means the selling price of the goods *includes* transportation costs to the specific location named in the contract. Shipments may be sent FOB *destination* or FOB *shipment*, and any risk of loss is determined based on which of these two options is chosen.

- *FOB destination* - With this shipping option, the seller assumes the risk of loss until the goods are delivered by them to the buyer's store or warehouse. The buyer must be notified the goods arrived at the destination and be given a reasonable time to pick them up. This option is also referred to as a 'destination contract.'

- *FOB shipment* - With this shipping option, terms of the contract require the seller to ship the goods by carrier without any particular destination stated, and the risk of loss passes to the buyer as soon as the seller delivers the goods to the carrier. This option is also referred to as a 'shipment contract.'

Sale on approval - A sale on approval exists when goods are delivered to a buyer with the understanding they can be returned if the buyer is not satisfied after having the opportunity to examine or test the goods before making the purchase. These sales may be referred to as a 'sale on trial,' and the goods are delivered to the buyer for a stated period of time. The seller retains title and risk of loss until the buyer actually accepts the goods.

Approval can be deemed as having occurred if the buyer acts in a manner inconsistent with a sale on trial or fails to state their approval or disapproval within the time period specified – or within a reasonable time if no time is specified – in the contract. Goods are subject to claims of the seller's **creditors** until the buyer's acceptance. Once the buyer accepts the goods, they are subject to the claims of the buyer's creditors.

Sale or return - In a sale or return contract for goods, the buyer purchases goods for the purpose of reselling them but may return those goods if the resale does not occur. The right to return must be set forth in a written contract, and the goods must be returned within the time period stated in the contract – or if not stated, within a reasonable time – and the goods must be in substantially the same condition as when originally received. The buyer bears the risk of loss until the goods are returned to the seller, and the goods are subject to the buyer's creditors while in the buyer's possession.

Warranties

The purpose of a **warranty** is to protect a consumer (purchaser) by giving them an assurance the article, good, or service will be in conformity with a certain standard or operate in a certain manner. A warranty states the seller agrees to make good on any loss or damage the purchaser may experience if the goods are not as represented. When a warranty is made *at the time of sale*, it is considered to be part of the contractual agreement and binding on the parties. A warranty made *after the sale* is also binding on the parties and considered a *modification* of the sales contract.

The **Uniform Commercial Code** requires a *warranty of title*, meaning the seller must convey a valid title to the goods and assert the transfer is rightful. In addition, the seller must also warrant the goods will be delivered free of any claim by the seller's creditors for which the buyer has no knowledge.

The UCC also requires a *warranty against infringement*, meaning the seller must warrant goods will be delivered free of the rightful claims of any third person by way of a patent or trademark infringement. An exception to this warranty occurs when the seller supplies goods according to specifications furnished by the buyer. Under those circumstances, the buyer must hold the seller harmless from any infringement claim arising out of the seller's compliance with the specifications.

Express Warranties

An **express warranty** is the actual and definite statement of a seller – either orally or in writing – at the time of the sale. This relates specifically to a seller's affirmation of fact or promise that relates to the goods and becomes the basis of the bargain. A seller can create an express warranty by making representations regarding the condition, quality, description, or performance potential of the goods. A seller's opinions or puffing – a mere expression of an opinion – does not create an express warranty. Descriptions, samples, and models of the goods may create an express warranty, as the seller does not need to state any particular words to make such a warranty.

When an express warranty is breached, the seller is absolutely liable. Disclaimers of express warranties are not favored, and any attempt to disclaim an express warranty fails if the disclaimer is inconsistent with the warranty. A seller can disclaim oral express warranties by including a written disclaimer in the contract that is stated in clear language, conspicuous, and called to the buyer's attention. The buyer must be made aware of any disclaimers or modifications at the time the contract is formed.

Implied Warranties

Implied warranties are imposed by law and arise automatically when a sale takes place. Funeral establishments provide implied warranties when they sell goods, even though they do not manufacture the goods. The most common implied warranties are set forth below.

Warranty of merchantability - This implied warranty only applies to a **merchant** seller in that the goods sold are fit for the ordinary purposes for which they are being sold. A merchant in this case is defined as a person who deals in goods of the kind or otherwise by occupation purports to have knowledge or skill peculiar to the practices or goods involved in the transaction. Funeral directors are considered merchants as they deal in special goods and merchandise – such as caskets, vaults and urns – and, by their occupation are expected and assumed to have more knowledge than others about these particular goods.

Products subject to a warranty of merchantability must:

- conform to the standards of the trade;
- be fit for the purpose the goods are ordinarily used;
- uniform as to quality and quantity; and
- meet the specifications on any package labels.

If a product has an implied warranty of merchantability and it does not meet its intended purpose, there are legal remedies available to the consumer.

Warranty of fitness for a particular purpose - This implied warranty arises when a seller – merchant or otherwise – knows of the particular purpose for which a buyer will use the goods and the buyer is relying on the skill and judgement of the seller to select suitable goods. The warranty is usually implied through the salesperson's assurance or recommendation of an item for a specific purpose.

For example, if a funeral director assures a consumer an urn holds up to 200 cubic inches of cremated remains and it turns out the maximum capacity is less than 200 cubic inches, the urn could be returned to the seller under the implied warranty of fitness.

Unless properly disclaimed, funeral directors may be liable for defective or faulty merchandise. To avoid complications with implied warranties, funeral establishments should rely on and refer to the manufacturer descriptions, information, and warranty when speaking with consumers.

In the urn example, the funeral director could tell the buyer that *according to the manufacturer of the urn* it holds a minimum of 200 cubic inches of cremated remains, rather than assuring the buyer it will hold that amount and thereby implying the funeral director – not the manufacturer – is making the representation.

Warranty arising from circumstances or usage of trade - When both parties have knowledge of a well-recognized trade custom – which amounts to the usual way of doing things – courts may infer both parties intended the trade custom to apply to their contract.

<u>Magnuson-Moss Warranty Act</u>
This legislation was enacted to deal with many different kinds of abuses relating to warranties when dealing with consumers. The Act applies only when written warranties are made voluntarily on consumer products that cost more than $25. Warranties on these products must be clearly disclosed to the buyer and labeled as either 'full' or 'limited.'

The Act directed the Federal Trade Commission to:

- develop regulations for written warranties;
- establish disclosure standards for written warranties;
- limit disclaimer of implied warranties; and
- establish consumer remedies for breach of warranty or **service contract** obligations.

Disclaimer of warranties - A warranty disclaimer is a statement that informs a buyer the seller is not bound by any warranty guarantees or promises regarding the product. Funeral establishments may disclaim warranties by means of a statement that uses specific language and is presented to the consumer in a clear and conspicuous manner.

Funeral directors are cautioned to carefully review state laws, as some states may prohibit a disclaimer of implied warranties. The Uniform Commercial Code (UCC) provides a warranty disclaimer regarding an implied warranty of merchantability must mention the word merchantability and must be conspicuous.

The UCC also provides:

> *All implied warranties are excluded by expressions like 'as is' 'with all faults' or other language which in common understanding calls the buyer's attention to the exclusion of warranties and makes plain that there is no implied warranty.*

A typical disclaimer of warranties statement that may be used by a funeral establishment is provided here as an example. However, funeral establishment owners and operators should always consult with an attorney in developing a disclaimer that complies with both the Magnuson-Moss Warranty Act and any applicable laws in those states where they offer funeral goods to the public.

Disclaimer of Warranties

XYZ Funeral Home makes no representations or warranties regarding the caskets, vaults, urns, or other goods and merchandise we offer. We do not warrant or claim that any casket or vault we offer is airtight and/or watertight. We do not claim that any casket or vault we offer has preservative qualities.

Our funeral establishment hereby expressly disclaims all warranties, expressed or implied, relating to the merchandise we offer, including but not limited to, the implied warranties of merchantability and fitness for a particular purpose.

The only warranties, expressed or implied, granted in connection with the merchandise we offer are the express written warranties, if any, granted by the manufacturer of the goods and merchandise.

Display of manufacturer warranty - The Act also provides the seller of a consumer product with a written manufacturer warranty must make the text of the warranty readily available for examination by a prospective buyer. This may be accomplished in either of two ways:

1. Displaying it in close proximity to the warranted product. This includes through electronic or other means if the manufacturer has elected to use an accessible digital format on the manufacturer's website.

2. Furnishing it upon request *prior* to the sale (including through electronic or other means) and placing signs in prominent locations reasonably calculated to elicit the prospective buyer's attention and advise them of the availability of warranties upon request.

To avoid any sense of offering or sharing responsibility for a warranty with a manufacturer, funeral establishments can refrain from making any claims as to the qualities, abilities, or capabilities of a product without expressly stating product attributes and guarantees are warranted by the manufacturer, *not* the funeral director or the funeral establishment.

Chapter 9: Consumer Protections - Part 1

Overview

This chapter is the first of two that explore business law from the viewpoint of protections afforded to consumers under federal and state statutes. This first chapter includes information on: regulatory agencies that enforce consumer protection laws; the federal Truth-in-Lending Act; and the FTC Funeral Rule.

Note: Definitions for selected terms are provided within the sections to which they apply.

Regulatory Agencies

Federal - The majority of federal codes, rules, and acts with respect to consumer protections are under the jurisdiction of the Federal Trade Commission (FTC) and/or the Consumer Product Safety Commission (CPSC). This chapter includes those regulated by the FTC; while the following chapter includes those regulated by the CPSC. Special attention is given in this chapter to the FTC Funeral Rule that specifically regulates the funeral service industry.

State and local - In addition to federal codes, rules, and acts that influence and regulate funeral service businesses, states have numerous laws and countless administrative rules and regulations to control and manage the operation of funeral establishments and the conduct of funeral directors. These regulations are of course state specific, with no two states having identical requirements. In many cases, state laws have expanded on the FTC Funeral Rule, especially as it relates to consumer protections.

Larger metropolitan areas, such as New York City, also regulate funeral services within their jurisdiction. For example, in the city a local law requires funeral establishments have copies of their GPL clearly visible and easily accessible in all areas of the funeral service establishment where sales or potential sales of funeral services are discussed. In addition, NYC requires they be clearly visible and easily accessible in the immediate vicinity of the main public entrance to the funeral establishment. The FTC Funeral Rule has no similar requirements. And, for New York establishments *not* located in NYC, owners only need to provide a GPL to a consumer at the time of the arrangement conference, as required by the federal Rule.

Truth-in-Lending Act

The federal Truth in Lending Act (TILA) protects consumers against inaccurate and unfair credit billing and credit card practices. It requires **creditors** (lenders) to provide consumers with loan cost information so they can comparison shop for certain loans. For those funeral establishments that offer to finance the purchase of funeral goods and services – and meet the definition of a creditor – the Act requires them to provide standard disclosures about the terms of the financing.

Creditor - Not all funeral establishments will meet the definition of a creditor that triggers the requirement to comply with the Act. Creditor is defined as:

> *... a person who* ***regularly*** *extends consumer credit that is subject to a finance charge or is payable by written agreement in more than four installments (not including a down payment), and to whom the obligation is initially payable, either*

on the face of the note or contract, or by agreement when there is no note or contract. [**Bold** emphasis added.]

A 'person' in this definition includes any type of business or entity.

When a funeral establishment offers to extend credit subject to finance charges or payable in more than four installments, they are – for the purposes of the Act – extending consumer credit. However, a funeral establishment '*regularly*' extends consumer credit only if it does so more than 25 times in a preceding calendar year, or more than 25 times in any current year if it did not exceed this number in the preceding year.

Consumer - For the purposes of TILA, a consumer is defined as a *natural person* to whom consumer credit is offered or extended. The requirements of the Act would not apply to a creditor (i.e., a funeral establishment) when the obligator on the funeral contract is a not a natural person, such as a company, charity, corporation, executor, trustee, or fiduciary.

General disclosure requirements - If an establishment meets the definition of a creditor, they must provide consumers with mandatory disclosures and meet several requirements, including:

Format. A funeral establishment must provide the disclosures required by the Act clearly and conspicuously in writing and in a form that the consumer may keep. They may be provided to the consumer in electronic form, subject to compliance with the consumer's consent and federal regulations.

Acknowledgements - Disclosures may include an acknowledgment of receipt, the date of the transaction, and the consumer's name, address, and account number.

Time of Disclosures - The funeral establishment must make the required disclosures before concluding the transaction.

Basis of Disclosures and Use of Estimates - Disclosures must reflect the terms of the legal obligation between the parties. If any information necessary for an accurate disclosure is unknown to a funeral establishment at the time, they must make the disclosure based on the best information reasonably available at the time the disclosure is provided to the consumer and must clearly state the disclosure is an estimate.

Multiple Consumers - If a transaction involves more than one consumer, the disclosures may be made to any consumer who is primarily liable on the obligation.

Standard disclosures - The Act specifies the standard disclosures that must – when applicable – be provided to the consumer when extending consumer credit. These disclosures must be provided to the consumer on a separate document or form. They may not be included on the required FTC Statement, a funeral contract, or other similar funeral agreement, and must be provided to the consumer *before* the execution of the funeral agreement. These include the following disclosures.

Creditor. The name and identity of the creditor making the disclosures.

Amount Financed. This disclosure must be styled as 'Amount Financed' and include a brief description, such as the amount of credit provided to the consumer. The amount financed is calculated by:

- determining the principal loan amount or the cash price (subtracting any down payment);
- adding any other amounts that are financed by the creditor and are not part of the finance charge; and
- subtracting any prepaid finance charge.

Itemization of Amount Financed. There must be a separate disclosure with a written itemization of the amount financed, including:

- the amount of any proceeds distributed directly to the consumer;
- the amount credited to the consumer's account with the creditor; and
- any amounts paid to other persons by the creditor on the consumer's behalf. This section would require a funeral establishment to disclose all cash advances paid on behalf of the consumer, including the name of the person paid and the goods or services provided.

A creditor does not need to comply with the third section of this disclosure if they provide a statement that the consumer has the right to receive a written itemization of the amount financed, together with a space for the consumer to indicate whether it is desired, and the consumer elects not to request an itemization.

Finance Charge. This disclosure must be styled as 'Finance Charge' and include a brief description, such as 'the dollar amount the credit will cost you.'

Annual Percentage Rate. This disclosure must be styled as 'Annual Percentage Rate,' and include a brief description, such as 'the cost of your credit as a yearly rate.'

Payment Schedule. This schedule must include the number, amounts, and timing of payments scheduled to repay the obligation.

Total of Payments. This disclosure must be styled as 'Total of Payments,' and include a descriptive explanation, such as 'the amount you will have paid when you have made all scheduled payments.'

Total Sale Price. This disclosure must be styled as 'Total Sale Price' and include a descriptive explanation, such as 'the total price of your purchase on credit, including your down payment of $_________.' The total sale price is the sum of the cash price, any other amounts financed by the creditor and not part of the finance charge, and the finance charge disclosed under the finance charge section.

Prepayment. A consumer must be notified if there is a penalty if the obligation is prepaid in full; and conversely, if the funeral establishment offers a rebate for prepayment in full, the consumer must be notified in the disclosure.

Late Payment. Any charges imposed due to late payment must be included in the disclosures.

Security Interest. If the funeral establishment will acquire a security interest in the property purchased as a part of the transaction, or any other property, it must be disclosed and identified by item or type.

Prefunded preneeds - Preneed funeral arrangements are subject to the same provisions of TILA as at-need funeral arrangements. If a funeral establishment requires any type of finance charge or permits the consumer to pay for the preneed in more than four installments in accordance with a written agreement, they would be required to comply with the Act if they extend such credit more than 25 times in a year, as previously defined.

Late charges - Late charges are not considered to be 'finance charges' as defined under the Act. It is therefore very important funeral establishments do not label late charges on the FTC Statement – or other written agreements for the purchase of funeral goods and services – as interest payments, finance charges, or other similarly worded phrases that might be considered a finance charge under the Act. They are simply 'late charges.'

Advertising - If an advertisement for credit states specific credit terms, it must state only those terms that actually are or will be arranged or offered by the creditor. They must be made clearly and conspicuously. If an advertisement states a rate of finance charge, it must state the rate as an 'annual percentage rate.' If the annual percentage rate may be increased after the credit agreement has been executed, the advertisement must also state this fact.

Record retention - A funeral establishment must retain evidence of compliance with TILA regulations for two years after the date disclosures are required to be made or action is required to be taken. They must also permit any agency responsible for enforcing the regulations to inspect relevant records for compliance.

Federal Trade Commission

The mission of the Federal Trade Commission (FTC) is to protect consumers and competition by preventing anticompetitive, deceptive, and unfair business practices through law enforcement, advocacy, and education without unduly burdening legitimate business activity.

The FTC, Federal Regulation Rule for Funeral Industry Practices is the one federal statute that specifically addresses funeral services. Known simply as the Funeral Rule, it has significant regulatory compliance requirements for funeral service owners, operators, and practitioners.

The purpose of the Funeral Rule is to provide certain rights to consumers when making funeral arrangements, either at the time when death occurs or when making arrangements in advance of need. The Funeral Rule specifically prohibits funeral directors from:

- misrepresenting legal, crematory, and cemetery requirements;
- embalming for a fee without permission;
- requiring the purchase of a casket for direct cremation; and
- requiring consumers to buy certain funeral goods or services as a condition for furnishing other funeral goods or services.

In practice, the Funeral Rule allows consumers to comparison shop for prices from any number of different funeral establishments. With this pricing information in hand, consumers can make an informed decision on which establishment they want to provide them with funeral goods and services.

The Funeral Rule is centered around provisions that require funeral directors to provide consumers with accurate, up-to-date, itemized price lists and information. The three price lists mandated by the Funeral Rule are a general price list, casket price list, and outer burial container price list. Another provision of the Funeral Rule requires funeral directors to provide consumers with a Statement of Funeral Goods and Services Selected at the conclusion of the arrangement conference.

<u>General Price List</u>
A printed or typewritten General Price List (GPL) must be given to all individuals who inquire *in person* about the funeral goods, funeral services, or prices of funeral goods or services offered by a funeral establishment. A funeral director must provide the list to a consumer upon beginning discussion of any of the following:

1. The prices of funeral goods or funeral services;
2. The overall type of funeral service or disposition; or
3. Specific funeral goods or funeral services offered by the funeral provider.

These three activities are referred to as triggering events, or face-to-face meetings that then require a funeral director to give the consumer a GPL for review and retention (to keep).

Who can get the list? - Funeral establishment competitors, news media representatives, clergy members, government officials, and consumer advocacy groups are just a few of the possible individuals or groups that may request a GPL. There are *no exceptions* to who can get a GPL. Anyone and everyone can request a GPL and must by law be given one.

Information from the required price lists must be provided to those who telephone a funeral establishment and inquire about the price of funeral goods and funeral services, but the rule does not require funeral establishments to mail or otherwise provide callers with a GPL based on a telephone call. However, there is also nothing in the rule to prohibit a funeral establishment from mailing a GPL to someone if they choose to do so. Some states may have rules and regulations that do *require* a GPL be mailed upon request.

A GPL cannot be shown in a booklet or binder where it appears there is only one copy available. An individual hard copy must be physically offered to consumers so they can take it home with them when they leave. A consumer does not have to accept or review a GPL, and a funeral director is not required to do anything beyond offering and making one available to them. However, a funeral director also may not do or say anything to discourage a consumer from accepting, reviewing, or keeping a GPL. Additionally, no fees or conditions may be set for a consumer to receive a GPL, as they must be provided free of charge.

Information required - A GPL must contain at least the following information in the heading:

1. The name, address, and telephone number of the funeral provider's place of business;

2. A caption describing the list as a 'General Price List'; and

3. The effective date of the list.

The effective date is the date on which the GPL is first made available to be given or offered to persons requesting funeral service information.

Following the heading, a GPL must itemize *16 specific items of goods and services*, together with the price for each item. Itemization – the pricing method used on a GPL – is a method of listing goods and services that treats each individual good or service being offered as a separate line item that includes the price for the item.

In addition to the 16 specific items, there are *six disclosures* required in the rule that must be included within the itemized listings. These disclosures must use the identical wording provided in the rule and be located in specific locations. Additional information, such as state laws or regulations relevant to an item may be added, but a funeral establishment can not change the FTC language or add anything that would modify the FTC language.

<u>Casket Price List</u>
Casket prices may be included on and made a part of the General Price List, or in the alternative be provided on a separate casket price list (CPL). When using a separate casket price list, the list must provide the following basic information:

1. The name of the business (funeral establishment).

2. A caption describing the list as a Casket Price List.

3. The effective date for the price list.

4. The retail price of each casket and alternative container that does not require special ordering, along with enough information to identify them.

Alternative containers - If a funeral establishment offers direct cremation as a service option, they must also offer at least one direct cremation selection that includes an alternative container. The prices of alternative containers must be listed together with the caskets on the CPL. Caskets may not be on one list and alternative containers on a different list.

Item descriptions - Descriptions of the different caskets and alternative containers must be sufficient enough to clearly identify them. The rule does not go into any detail on what the descriptions must include, but most states require any or all of the following:

- the make, model, and name of the casket or alternative container;
- a description of the interior cloth weave and style, such as a velvet, crepe (rhymes with cape), or satin weave; and a tailored, shirred (rhymes with bird), or tufted style;
- the exterior finish, such as polished, brushed, painted, natural, or cloth-covered;
- the gauge of metal, for metal caskets; and
- the species of wood, for wooden caskets.

Providing a photograph or simply a manufacturer name and model are not sufficient to identify a casket or alternative container.

Format - The Funeral Rule does not require any particular format for the list, nor is there any requirement on the order in which caskets and alternative containers must be placed on the list. It may be in any form, including in a notebook or on a chart as long as it contains the required information. All of the CPL information must be displayed in a clear and conspicuous manner.

Some states and localities have adopted very specific formatting requirements for a CPL that must be complied with by funeral service practitioners that operate within those jurisdictions.

Providing the list - A funeral establishment must give a CPL for review to anyone who asks *in person* about the caskets or alternative containers they offer or the prices they charge for them. The list must be offered to a consumer when discussions *begin* about caskets or alternative containers. The offer must be made *prior* to showing any caskets or alternative containers to a consumer, thereby providing them the opportunity to look at the price list before discussing the options or viewing the actual products.

The FTC is very specific in stating consumers should not first learn of casket prices by entering a casket showroom or selection room and reading price cards placed on individual caskets, or by having the funeral director recite price information to them orally. A funeral establishment may use individual price cards on caskets and containers, but this pricing method must be *in addition to* having a CPL.

For funeral establishments that use a manufacturer or supplier casket showroom outside the funeral establishment facility, they must offer the CPL when and where the discussion of casket offerings and prices begins. This may occur at the funeral establishment, if this is where discussions begin; or at the manufacturer or supplier casket showroom, if this is where the discussion begins.

The casket price list must be given to a consumer for *review*, but it does not need to be given to them to keep, as is required for a General Price List; however, there is no prohibition on allowing a consumer to keep the CPL if the funeral establishment wants to do so.

Display - The Funeral Rule does not require caskets or containers be displayed in any specific manner or arrangement, and there are no requirements to have caskets and containers on display if a funeral establishment does not want or have the necessary space to do so. Some establishments present selections by using a book containing photographs of the various caskets and containers they offer.

When using a book, catalog, or other media format for presentations, it must include all the information required for a CPL, including the business name, a caption describing the presentation materials as a Casket Price List, and the effective date of the list.

Some states or municipalities may have display requirements, such as having lower priced units displayed in a similar fashion and location to higher priced units.

<u>Outer Burial Container Price List</u>
The Funeral Rule does not require a funeral establishment offer outer burial containers. However, if they do offer these containers, they must have an outer burial container price list (OBCPL) for consumers to review that provides the following basic information:

1. The name of the business (funeral establishment).

2. A caption describing the list as an Outer Burial Container Price List.

3. The effective date for the price list.

4. The retail price of each outer burial container that does not require special ordering, and enough information to identify them.

5. The mandatory Funeral Rule disclosure for an outer burial container price list.

Item descriptions - Descriptions must be sufficient enough to clearly identify the items listed. The Funeral Rule does not go into any detail on what the descriptions must include, but most states require any or all of the following:

- the name of the supplier;

- the name of the manufacturer;
- the model name or number; and
- a description of the construction material, such as concrete, carbon steel, stainless steel, copper, aluminum, or polymer (plastic) derivatives.

Providing a photograph or simply a manufacturer name and model are not sufficient to identify an outer burial container.

Disclosure - The following disclosure must be included on an OBCPL:

> *[In most areas of the country], [S]tate or local law does not require that you buy a container to surround the casket in the grave. However, many cemeteries require that you have such a container so that the grave will not sink in. Either a grave liner or a burial vault will satisfy these requirements.*

If no state or local law requires an outer burial container – such as a burial vault – surround a casket in the grave, the Funeral Rule allows a funeral establishment to delete the phrase [in most areas of the country] from the disclosure. The first sentence of the disclosure would then read: *State or local law does not require that you buy a container to surround the casket in the grave.*

Providing the list - A funeral establishment must give an OBCPL for review to anyone who asks *in person* about the outer burial containers they offer or the prices they charge for them. The list must be offered to a consumer when discussions *begin* about outer burial containers. The offer must be made *prior* to showing any outer burial containers to a consumer, thereby providing them the opportunity to look at the price list before discussing the options or viewing the actual products. A funeral establishment may use individual price cards on outer burial containers or models of miniature containers, but this pricing method must be *in addition to* having the required price list.

The outer burial container price list must be given to a consumer for *review*, but it does not need to be given to them to keep, as is required for a General Price List; however, there is no prohibition on allowing a consumer to keep an OBCPL if the funeral establishment wants to do so.

Display - The Funeral Rule does not require outer burial containers be displayed in any specific manner or arrangement, and there are no requirements to have outer burial containers on display if a funeral establishment does not want or have the necessary space to have an outer burial selection showroom. Some establishments present selections by using a book containing photographs of the various outer burial containers they offer. When using a book, catalog, or other media format for presentations, it must include all the information required for an OBCPL, including the business name, a caption describing the presentation materials as an Outer Burial Container Price List, the mandatory Funeral Rule disclosure, and the effective date of the list.

<u>Statement of Funeral Goods and Services Selected</u>
Following arrangements, the Funeral Rule requires a funeral establishment provide the consumer with a Statement of Funeral Goods and Services Selected (Statement). The purpose of the Statement is to allow the consumer to evaluate selections they made and make any desired changes.

When to provide - If the funeral arrangements take place in person, the Statement must be given to the consumer at the conclusion of the arrangements. It is not acceptable to mail or give the Statement to the consumer on a later date or time. In those cases where arrangements are made by telephone, the consumer must be given the Statement at the earliest possible date. If all of the arrangements are made by telephone and the consumer is not going to visit the funeral establishment before the final disposition takes place, the Statement should be given or sent to the consumer as soon as possible.

Format - The Funeral Rule does not require any specific form, heading, or caption on the Statement. The information required may be included on a contract or other similar type written document; however, it should be noted many states have laws that require a specific form and format be used to meet the Funeral Rule requirement for a Statement.

Funeral home charges - All of the goods and services selected by the consumer must be listed on the Statement, and the listing must correspond to the items and order as listed on the GPL. Each item must be listed separately with the price, along with any disclosure required by the Funeral Rule. Similar to the requirements for a GPL, package pricing is allowed as long as they are offered *in addition to*, not in place of, itemized prices for each of the items in the package. If the consumer selects a package, the Statement should describe the package by listing each of the individual goods and services that are included and then state the package price.

Cash advance charges - Cash advance items are items of service or merchandise that:

- are described to a consumer as a 'cash advance,' 'accommodation,' 'cash disbursement,' or similar term; or

- are obtained from a third party and paid for by the funeral establishment on behalf of the consumer.

Cash advance items *may* include such items as cemetery or crematory services, pallbearers, public transportation, clergy honoraria, flowers, musicians or singers, obituary notices, gratuities, and death certificates. When the price for a cash advance item is not immediately known, the funeral establishment must enter a good faith estimate; however, a written statement of the actual charges with no estimates must be provided to the consumer before the final bill is paid. Each cash advance item selected must be listed on the Statement with the price.

Total funeral expenses - The Statement must include the total cost of the funeral arrangements selected by the consumer, including the cost of the goods and services (funeral home charges), plus any cash advance items (cash advance charges).

Funeral home charges + Cash advance charges = Total cost of funeral arrangements

Required disclosures - There are three Funeral Rule disclosures that must be on the Statement, and they must use the identical wording provided in the rule. Additional information, such as state laws or regulations relevant to the item may be included, but a funeral establishment may not change the FTC language or add anything that would modify the FTC language. The three disclosures address: legal requirements, embalming, and cash advances.

The legal requirements disclosure informs a consumer they will only be charged for the items they selected, or were required by law, or were required by a cemetery or crematory. And further, the funeral establishment will explain those legal, cemetery, or crematory requirements in writing.

The disclosure reads as follows:

> *Charges are only for those items that you selected or that are required. If we are required by law or by a cemetery or crematory to use any items, we will explain the reasons in writing below.*

The embalming disclosure is related to the need to have prior approval to embalm human remains. The disclosure reads as follows:

> *If you selected a funeral that may require embalming, such as a funeral with viewing, you may have to pay for embalming. You do not have to pay for embalming you did not approve if you selected arrangements such as a direct cremation or immediate burial. If we charged for embalming, we will explain why below.*

The cash advance disclosure is required when a funeral establishment has chosen to make a profit on cash advances. The Funeral Rule does not prohibit a funeral establishment from adding a service charge (profit) to a cash advance item or require disclosure to the consumer of the amount of the service charge. However, if a service charge is to be collected, or the funeral establishment retains a rebate, commission, or trade or volume discount for a cash advance item, the disclosure is required.

Disclosures must be placed in immediate conjunction with (directly next to) the list of cash advance items on the Statement, and specify the items to which the disclosure applies. This disclosure cannot be on a separate page or elsewhere on the Statement apart from the list of itemized cash advance items, and must read as follows:

> *We charge you for our services in obtaining*: ______________________________

It is important to note, each of the 50 states may *expand* on the funeral rule requirements in their home state. As an example, some states prohibit a funeral establishment from making any profit whatsoever on a cash advance, while other states have laws that enumerate those items which *must* be cash advance items and cannot be listed as a funeral home charge.

Larger metropolitan areas, such as New York City and Los Angeles County, may also regulate funeral services.

Note: The author has not reviewed the FTC Funeral Rule here in great detail as it goes beyond the scope of this book. The topic is explored extensively in college textbooks adopted for use in law courses of instruction found in funeral service programs across the nation. The second edition of *Funeral Service Law in the United States*, most recently revised in 2022 is one such source. Additional information about this book may be found in the Sources Consulted listing.

Chapter 10: Consumer Protections - Part 2

Overview

This chapter is the second of two that explore business law from the perspective of protections afforded to consumers under federal and state statutes. This chapter reviews usury laws, the Fair Credit reporting Act, product safety laws; antitrust laws; and truth in advertising laws.

Note: Definitions for selected terms are provided within the sections to which they apply.

Usury Laws

Usury laws define the maximum interest rate that may legally be charged on a loan. When an interest rate exceeds the maximum rate of interest which may be charged, the practice is called **usurious** and, in all 50 states – is illegal. There is no federal usury law, but each state has a statute that provides interest rate protections for consumers.

Usury laws vary and maximum interest rates may be different *within* a state based on the purpose of the financial agreement, such as those for credit cards, personal loans, car loans, or payroll loans. Larger corporations may charge the maximum interest rate allowed in the state in which they are incorporated rather than the state where the borrower resides. In some cases, this circumvents a lower rate in the borrower state, a practice that became legal following a U.S. Supreme Court ruling in 1978.

A borrower who has been charged an interest rate that violates a state usury law may initiate a civil claim against the lender to recover the excessive amount paid for interest above the allowable rate (compensatory damages). They may also be entitled to punitive damages which could – in some states – include the application of all payments made (principal and interest) toward the principal balance. In other states, the penalty could include awards in an amount double or triple the excessive amount the consumer was overcharged.

A lender who has repeatedly offered loans with inflated interest rates to certain classes of individuals or entities may be charged civilly by a state attorney general or other government official. In addition, there are some aggravating factors that may give rise to the filing of criminal charges against an offender. These factors may include such matters as the number of consumers that have fallen victim to the misconduct of one particular lender or the imposition of excessively high interest rates.

Some states, such as California, exempt all licensed lending institutions – banks, savings and loan, credit unions, and finance companies – from compliance with their usury laws.

Individuals who charge an excessive interest rate are often referred to derogatorily as loan sharks. Loan sharks are usually associated with unlicensed lenders that target and lend money to individuals with a low income that are unable to secure a loan through traditional lenders. These lenders (sharks) may be part of a larger criminal enterprise and are often found in major metropolitan areas.

Fair Credit Reporting Act
The Fair Credit Reporting Act promotes the accuracy, fairness, and privacy of information in the files of consumer reporting agencies. There are many types of consumer reporting agencies, including credit bureaus and agencies that sell information about check writing histories, medical records, and rental history records. The three major consumer credit reporting agencies in the United States are Equifax, Experian, and TransUnion.

Businesses, such as a funeral establishment, that provide information to consumer reporting agencies have requirements under the Act. Known as 'information furnishers,' these businesses are responsible for:

- reporting accurate financial information to consumer reporting agencies;
- promptly correcting any inaccurate information previously provided;
- advising consumers within 30 days of any negative information being reported; and
- having procedures for responding to identity theft notices sent by consumer reporting agencies.

Product Safety Laws
Product safety laws in the United States are a collection of codes and rules regulated primarily by the Consumer Product Safety Commission (CPSC). Deaths, injuries, and property damage from consumer product incidents cost the United States more than $1 trillion annually.

The CPSC is charged with protecting the public from unreasonable risks of injury or death associated with the use of the thousands of types of consumer products under the agency's jurisdiction. The CPSC is committed to protecting consumers and families from products that pose a fire, electrical, chemical, or mechanical hazard. The work of the CPSC to ensure the safety of consumer products – such as toys, cribs, power tools, cigarette lighters, and household chemicals – has contributed to a decline in the rate of deaths and injuries associated with consumer products over the past 40 years.

For example, many funeral establishments sell various types of memorial candles, candle holders, and candle accessories when making funeral arrangements, and the CPSC has guidelines relevant to the sale of candles and associated products. Guidelines include information on such topics as: cautionary labels for burning candles; specifications for glass candle holders; fire safety for candles; and candle emissions.

The following provides four examples of products the CPSC monitors and regulates.

Flammable Fabrics Act - This act regulates the manufacture of highly flammable clothing and interior furnishings. Some examples of standards passed and established by CPSC are for clothing textiles, vinyl plastic film used in clothes, carpets and rugs, children's sleepwear, mattresses, and mattress pads.

Children's Gasoline Burn Prevention Act - This act requires portable gasoline containers manufactured for sale in the United States on or after January 17, 2009, to conform to safety requirements for child resistant packaging.

Federal Hazardous Substance Act - This act requires certain hazardous household products to have warning labels. It gives CPSC the authority to regulate or ban a hazardous substance – in addition to toys or other articles intended for use by children – under certain circumstances to protect the public. Examples of products regulated under this law include toys, cribs, rattles, pacifiers, bicycles, and bunk beds for children.

Refrigerator Safety Act - This act requires refrigerators to have a mechanism (usually a magnetic latch) that enables the refrigerator door to be opened from the inside in the event of accidental entrapment.

Note: Information for this listing of products was researched and developed from material published by the CPSC and available in various public communication mediums, including online.

Antitrust Laws

Antitrust laws seek to promote competition among businesses. They encompass several federal statutes. West's Encyclopedia of American Law describes the theory behind antitrust laws as follows:

> *The prevailing economic theory supporting antitrust laws in the United States is that the public is best served by free competition in trade and industry. When businesses fairly compete for the consumer's dollar, the quality of products and services increases while the prices decrease.*
>
> *However, many businesses would rather dictate the price, quantity, and quality of the goods that they produce, without having to compete for consumers. Some businesses have tried to eliminate competition through illegal means, such as fixing prices and assigning exclusive territories to different competitors within an industry. Antitrust laws seek to eliminate such illegal behavior and promote fee and fair marketplace competition.*

Antitrust laws proscribe unlawful mergers and business practices in general terms, leaving courts to decide which ones are illegal based on the facts of each case. Courts have applied the antitrust laws to changing markets from the late 19th century to the present digital age.

Antitrust laws have had the same basic objective for over 100 years to protect the process of competition for the benefit of consumers, making sure there are strong incentives for businesses to operate efficiently, keep prices down, and keep quality up.

Revisions have been made to these Acts over the years, but they remain the bedrock foundation of federal efforts to promote competition among businesses.

There are three primary federal antitrust laws:

1. The Sherman [Antitrust] Act (1890)
2. The Federal Trade Commission Act (1914)
3. The Clayton [Antitrust] Act (1914)

Note: The FTC has published summary descriptions of these three Acts, and the review that follows includes material and information from those summaries.

Sherman Act - The Sherman Act, often referred to as the Sherman Antitrust Act, outlaws "... *every contract, combination, or conspiracy in restraint of trade*," and any "*monopolization, attempted monopolization, or conspiracy or combination to monopolize*." In a 1911 Supreme Court ruling, the court established the Sherman Act does not prohibit every restraint of trade, only those that are *unreasonable*. This is known as the 'rule of reason' in antitrust cases.

An agreement by two people to form a partnership restrains trade but may not do so unreasonably, and therefore could be lawful under antitrust laws. To the contrary, certain acts are considered so harmful to competition that they are almost always illegal. These include agreements and arrangements between competing individuals or businesses to fix prices, divide markets, or rig bids. These acts are 'per se' violations of the Sherman Act. Black's Law Dictionary defines the 'per se rule' as the, "... *judicial principle that a trade practice violates the Sherman Act simply if the practice is a restraint of trade, regardless of whether it actually harms anyone*."

The penalties for violating the Sherman Act can be severe. Although most antitrust enforcement actions are civil, the Sherman Act is also a criminal law, and individuals and businesses that violate it may be prosecuted by the U.S. Department of Justice. Criminal prosecutions are typically limited to intentional and clear violations, such as when competitors fix prices or rig bids. The Sherman Act imposes criminal penalties of up to $100 million for a corporation and $1 million for an individual, together with up to 10 years in prison. Under federal law, the maximum fine may be increased to *twice* the amount the conspirators gained from the illegal acts or *twice* the money lost by the victims of the crime, if either of those amounts is over $100 million.

A Famous Sherman Act Case

AT&T is the longest standing telecommunications company in the United States. Although many smaller companies alleged that AT&T was **monopolizing** the market, the company enjoyed this unfettered status for many years. However, that began to change in 1974 after the Attorney General filed suit against the company. It would take seven years and four U.S. Attorney Generals later before there was a settlement of the case. AT&T agreed to be broken into seven different companies that would each be responsible for serving a different region of the country. Over time, five of these companies merged into AT&T incorporated while the other two are currently Verizon and Qwest. [**Bold** print added.]

Source: HG.org Legal Resources.

Federal Trade Commission Act (FTC Act) - The FTC Act prohibits, "*unfair methods of competition*" and "*unfair or deceptive acts or practices*." The Supreme Court has ruled all violations of the Sherman Act also violate the FTC Act. Therefore, although the FTC does not technically enforce the Sherman Act, it can bring cases against the same kind of activities that violate the Sherman Act. It also enforces other practices that may harm competition but which may not fit easily into categories of conduct formally prohibited by the Sherman Act.

When the FTC was created in 1914, its purpose was to prevent unfair methods of competition in commerce as part of an on-going battle at the time to break up monopolies and trusts. In subsequent years, Congress passed legislation giving the agency greater authority to police anticompetitive practices and administer other consumer protections. As a result, the FTC is responsible for such initiatives as the Telemarketing Sales Rule, Pay-Per-Call Rule, and Equal Credit Opportunity Act.

In 1975, Congress gave the FTC the responsibility of adopting industry-wide trade regulation rules, and the Funeral Rule is a direct result of this far-reaching authority.

FTC Enforcement of the Funeral Rule

In an April 2018 press release, the FTC reported investigators, working undercover in 11 states, found failures to disclose pricing information required by the Funeral Rule in 29 of the 134 funeral establishments they visited in 2017. This same press release provided insight into what the investigators were looking for by including this paragraph:

> *The FTC conducts undercover inspections to monitor funeral establishments' compliance with the Funeral Rule. The Rule gives consumers important rights when making funeral arrangements. For example, funeral establishments must provide consumers with an itemized general price list at the start of an in-person discussion of funeral arrangements, a casket price list before consumers view any caskets, and an outer burial container price list before they view grave liners or vaults.*
>
> *The Rule also prohibits funeral establishments from requiring consumers to buy any item, such as a casket, as a condition of obtaining any other funeral good or service. By requiring the provision of itemized prices, the Funeral Rule enables consumers to compare prices and buy only the goods and services they want.*

Clayton Act - The Clayton Act, sometimes referred to as the Clayton Antitrust Act, addresses specific practices the Sherman Act does not clearly prohibit, such as mergers and interlocking directorates (the same person making business decisions for competing companies). The Clayton Act prohibits mergers and acquisitions where the effect "*... may be substantially to lessen competition, or tend to create a monopoly*."

As amended by the Robinson-Patman Act of 1936, the Clayton Act also bans certain discriminatory prices, services, and allowances in dealings between merchants.

The Act authorizes private parties to sue for *triple* damages when they have been harmed by conduct that violates either the Sherman or Clayton Acts and to obtain a court order prohibiting the anticompetitive practice in the future.

Justice Department Alleges Clayton Act Antitrust Violations Against AT&T and Time Warner Merger

On November 20, 2017, the United States Justice Department, ... filed suit against media giants AT&T and Time Warner for a proposed merger worth nearly $85.4 billion. The Justice Department made its case in a 23-page complaint filed before the Federal District Court of the District of Columbia, arguing that the proposed vertical merger violates Section 7 of Clayton Antitrust Act of 1914.

AT&T, owner of DirecTV, arguably the nation's largest distributor of subscription television, seeks to obtain Time Warner, the owner of top TV networks like CNN, TNT, TBS, and HBO. The Justice Department alleges that the combined firm would likely *"use its control of Time Warner's popular programming as a weapon to harm competition."* Such a tactic, the Justice Department contends, violates antitrust law, specifically Section 7 of the Clayton Act.

For clarity, antitrust litigation focuses in part on the prevention of corporate monopolies, price-fixing, and corporate mergers likely to reduce competition in particular markets. Antitrust litigation primarily is driven by three federal laws: the Sherman Antitrust Act of 1890; the Clayton Act; and the Federal Trade Commission Act of 1914.

Source: Phil Raymond, Juris Magazine, December 2, 2017.
Note: Full article not reproduced.

State antitrust laws - In addition to federal statutes, most states have antitrust laws that are enforced by a state attorney general through civil litigation. These statutes are often based on federal antitrust laws and designed to strengthen or amplify consumer protections.

Truth in Advertising Laws

Truth-in-advertising laws in the United States are a collection of codes and rules primarily regulated by the Federal Trade Commission (FTC). Federal law requires advertisements to be truthful, not misleading, and when appropriate backed by scientific evidence.

The FTC enforces truth-in-advertising laws and applies the same standards no matter where an advertisement may appear – in newspapers and magazines, online, in the mail, or on billboards or buses. The FTC gives special attention to advertising claims that can affect the health of a consumer or their pocketbooks, such as claims about food, over-the-counter drugs, alcohol and tobacco, and dietary supplements.

When the FTC finds a case of fraud being carried out against consumers, they may file an action in a federal district court for an order to immediately and permanently stop the offender. Enforcement actions may also seek to freeze the assets of the offender and get compensation for victims.

A Truth-in-Advertising Case

In 2016, the Federal Trade Commission (FTC) filed a lawsuit against Volkswagen (VW), which claimed the car company had deceived customers with an advertising campaign it used to promote its supposedly 'Clean Diesel' vehicles. A year earlier, it had been exposed that VW had been cheating emissions tests on its diesel cars in the US for the past seven years.

The FTC alleged, *"Volkswagen deceived consumers by selling or leasing more than 550,000 diesel cars based on false claims that the cars were low-emission, environmentally friendly."*

During settlement negotiations, the FTC required Volkswagen to offer owners of any affected car two options: a buyback option or an approved modification to the vehicle's emission system.

In July of 2020, the FTC reported Volkswagen has successfully repaid buyers more than $9.5 billion under orders resulting from a targeted, misleading "clean diesel" advertising campaign.

Funeral establishments may be subject to monitoring and regulation by the FTC for any of their advertising activities. Of recent interest has been an increase in advertising for green or natural burials, as a growing number of consumers are looking to buy environmentally friendly 'green' products.

In 2017, the National Funeral Directors Association (NFDA) issued a press release that quoted from their 2017 Consumer Awareness and Preferences Study and reported:

> *Just over half of respondents (53.8%) said they would be interested in exploring green memorialization options to reduce the environmental impact of end-of-life rituals.*

In deference to this eco-friendly trend in the funeral service industry, companies have responded with 'green' marketing programs that tout the environmental benefits of the products they sell. However, there are times when what a company believes their green product claims mean and what the consumer believes they mean are two entirely different things. In response, the FTC has issued a set of *Green Guides* designed to help funeral service providers and other similarly situated marketers in eco-friendly green products avoid making environmental claims that could mislead consumers.

Another area in which truth-in-advertising laws may influence funeral home advertising is in the use of endorsements or testimonials. Endorsements are an important tool for advertisers and can be persuasive to consumers, but federal law requires these endorsements be truthful and not misleading. To assist advertisers and business owners in meeting this standard of truthfulness – regardless of the medium used to advertise or market a product or service – the FTC issued a set of guides.

Guides Concerning the Use of Endorsements and Testimonials in Advertising were developed to inform *advertisers* that that using unrepresentative testimonials may be misleading if they are not accompanied by information describing what consumers can generally expect from use of the product or service. Further, *endorsers* are advised they should not talk about their experience with a product if they have not tried it or make claims about a product that would require proof they do not have.

Note: FTC Guides are not regulations and there are no civil penalties associated with them; however, if advertisers do not follow the guides, the FTC may investigate whether practices are '*unfair or deceptive*' under the FTC Act, which could then result in sanctions and penalties.

Chapter 11: Uniform Commercial Code Article 3 - Part 1

Overview

This chapter reviews Article 3 of the Uniform Commercial Code as it relates to negotiable instruments, also known as commercial paper. The chapter begins with a review of classifications and requirements for negotiability and the different types of instruments used on a daily basis, such as checks and drafts. The chapter closes with a discussion on electronic fund transfers.

Chapter Definitions

Bearer - a person in possession of a negotiable instrument.

Bearer paper - Negotiable instrument payable to bearer or cash.

Cashier's check - A check drawn on a bank's own funds and signed by a responsible bank official.

Certificate of deposit (*CD*) - The acknowledgement by a bank of a receipt of money with an agreement of repayment.

Certified check - A check for which the bank assures that the drawer has sufficient funds to make payment.

Check - An order by a depositor on the bank to pay a sum of money to a payee.

Draft - A written order by one person directing another to pay a sum of money to a third person.

Drawee - The person, company or financial institution ordered to pay a draft.

Drawer - The person who executes any draft.

Maker - The party who executes a promissory note.

Negotiable instrument - A writing drawn in a special form which can be transferred as a substitute for money or as an instrument of credit.

Negotiation - The act of transferring ownership of a negotiable instrument to another party.

Order paper - Negotiable instrument made payable to the order of a named party; the word 'order' or its equivalent must be used.

Payee - The party to whom a negotiable instrument is made payable.

Promissory note - A negotiable instrument containing a promise to pay.

Negotiable Instruments

A **negotiable instrument** – also known as commercial paper – is a writing drawn in a special form which can be transferred from person to person as a substitute for money or as an instrument of credit. Most negotiable instruments are paper documents, which is why they are also referred to as commercial paper. As a substitute for money, a negotiable instrument is a powerful document because it can be passed on like money without fear it will not be uncollectible.

West's Encyclopedia of American Law describes commercial paper as:

> *A written instrument or document – such as a check, draft, promissory note, or a certificate of deposit – that manifests the pledge or duty of one individual to pay money to another.*
>
> *Commercial paper is ordinarily used in business transactions, since it is a reliable and expedient means of dealing with large sums of money and minimizes the risks inherent in using cash, such as the increased possibility of theft.*
>
> *One of the most significant aspects of commercial paper is that it is negotiable, which means that it can be freely transferred from one party to another, either through endorsement or delivery. The terms commercial paper and negotiable instrument can be used interchangeably.*

Commercial paper may be classified as either 'promises to pay' or 'orders to pay.'

<u>Promises to Pay</u>
Promissory note - A **promissory note** is a negotiable instrument containing a promise to pay. The money may be paid on demand or at a specific time. The person who executes a promissory note and agrees to pay a fixed amount of funds to the holder of the note is known as the **maker** of the note.

For example, Mary Smith signs a writing unconditionally promising to pay to the order of the First National Bank of Blackacre $5,000 with 5% interest by a certain date. This writing is a promissory note. Money is normally repaid with interest.

Certificate of deposit (CD) - A **certificate of deposit** is acknowledgement by a bank of the receipt of money with an agreement of repayment. The bank repays the money to the person designated on the CD on a certain date. A CD is a note of the bank and funds are repaid with interest.

For example, on March 1, John Jones deposits $5,000 with the Second National Bank of Blackacre. In return, the bank issues a CD to him in which it promises to repay the $5,000 plus interest six months later.

The party to whom any negotiable instrument is made payable is known as the **payee**.

<u>Orders to Pay</u>
Draft - A **draft** is a written order signed by one person directing another – often a financial institution – to pay a sum of money to a third person. The most common form of a draft document is a **check**, defined as an order by a depositor on their bank to pay a sum of money to a payee. The drawee of a draft must be reasonably named or identified.

For example, Frank writes and signs a personal check made out to Paul, thereby ordering his financial institution – Acme Bank – to pay Paul $100.

In this example:

- Frank is the **drawer**, a person who executes a draft (a personal check in this case);
- Acme Bank is the **drawee**, the institution on which the check is being drawn; and
- Paul is the payee, the party to whom a negotiable instrument is made payable.

Checks - As noted, checks are the most common form of a draft document. Checks are demand instruments because they are payable on demand. There are two special types of checks that are considered as trustworthy as cash:

1. *Certified check* - A **certified check** is a check for which the bank assures that the drawer has sufficient funds to make payment. When the check is certified, the bank immediately charges the account of the drawer with the amount of the check and transfers those funds to its own certified check account. This assures the funds to pay the check when it is cashed or deposited will be available and prevents the bank from denying liability.

2. *Cashier's check* - A **cashier's check** is drawn on the funds of the bank and signed by a responsible bank official. An individual can purchase a cashier's check from a bank by paying the face amount of the check together with a service fee for the bank issuing the check. The drawer does not need to have a checking account at the bank, and – once the check has been issued – it cannot be canceled.

<u>Requirements for Negotiability</u>

Negotiation is the act of transferring ownership of a negotiable instrument to another party. Negotiability refers to the form of an instrument, and there are six elements that must be present to demonstrate negotiability. The instrument must be:

1. In writing - A negotiable instrument must be written, but there is no requirement the writing be in any particular form. It may be written in pen, ink, or pencil; typed, printed, or handwritten.

2. Signed by a maker or drawer - A signature is required to demonstrate the intent of the promisor to be bound. Any name, mark, or other signature is sufficient so long as it is the intention to bind the party signing. Normally, the signature is placed in the lower right-hand corner of a check; however, the location is immaterial so long as a signature is intended.

   Signatures may be handwritten, typed, printed, or stamped but cannot be made on a separate piece of paper that is then attached to the instrument. The instrument may be signed by an authorized agent.

3. An unconditional order or promise to pay - A promise or order to pay must be unconditional. It cannot be a promise or order dependent on any condition or event that is not certain to occur. A promissory note must contain a *promise* to pay, and a draft must contain an *order* to pay. The acknowledgement of a debt is not considered a negotiable instrument, and the word 'promise' does not need to be used if the instrument's language shows a definite intent to pay.

4. State a fixed amount of money - The money specified in a written instrument does not have to be American currency; however, it must be in the form of some national medium of exchange that is legal tender at the place of payment. For example, it could be payable in dollars, yen, euros, pounds, pesos, or rubles.

   Payment cannot be in scrip (documents that entitle the holder to receive something of value), gold bullion, or bonds, but it can be in the payment of either money or goods. The instrument must state the principal sum and the amount or rate of interest to be paid. The amount cannot depend on future events or impose a duty to pay a sum that cannot be determined until sometime in the future.

5. Payable on demand or at a definite time - A payable on demand note stating '*on demand*' or payable '*at sight*' is called a sight draft and must be paid on presentation. If no time is stated on an instrument, it is considered to be payable on demand.

   If the instrument is to be paid in the future, the due date must be fixed. Additionally, an acceleration clause is allowed if the debtor fails to make one or more payments. Black's Law Dictionary defines acceleration as, "*The act or process of quickening or shortening the duration of something, such as payments or other functional activities*." A prepayment clause is also permitted that allows the debtor to make early payments toward the principal and/or interest.

6. Payable to order or to bearer, unless it is a check.

   Order paper is a commercial paper made payable to the order of some named party. The word 'order' or its equivalent must be used; however, the use of the word 'order' is usually preferred. Examples: 'pay to the order of James Jones' or 'pay to James Jones' or 'pay to James Jones or assignees.' The payee of an order paper must be reasonably named and identified.

   Bearer paper is a commercial paper payable to **bearer** or cash, i.e., to the person having possession of the writing. Examples are: 'pay to bearer' or 'pay to Dan Smith or bearer' or 'pay to cash.' There is an exception only with regard to checks, not other drafts or notes. If a check simply reads 'pay to Smith," the check is negotiable.

Electronic Fund Transfers

Banking in the 21st century has modernized the way the public does their banking business with the advent of electronic fund transfers (EFTs). EFTs are electronic transfers of money from one bank account to another – either within a single financial institution or across multiple institutions via computer-based systems – without the direct intervention of bank staff. The systems allow for the transfer of funds through the use of an electronic device, such as a terminal, telephone, computer, or cellphone.

The Electronic Fund Transfer Act (EFTA) is the federal law that regulates these systems and provides for the rights, liabilities, and responsibilities of users of EFT systems. Article 3 of the Uniform Commercial Code does not apply to these systems.

EFT Disclosure Requirements

Financial institutions are required to disclose the terms and conditions of an ETF involving a customer account at the time the service is contracted.

Required disclosures include but are not limited to:

- liabilities for unauthorized EFTs;
- types of EFTs customers may make; and
- fees for using EFTs.

Liabilities - If a customer's credit/debit card is lost or stolen and used without permission, the customer is obligated to pay no more than $50 if they notify the bank of the incident within two days of learning of the loss. For notifications made more than two days after a known loss, the liability increases to $500. A customer may be liable for more than $500 if they fail to report an unauthorized use within 60 days after it appears on their account statement.

A customer must discover any error on a monthly statement within 60 days, followed with notification to the bank. The bank then has ten days to investigate and must report its conclusions to the customer in writing. The bank must provide a monthly statement for every month in which there is an EFT on the statement.

Types of EFTs - A financial institution must disclose the types of EFTs a customer may make. EFT types may include automated teller machine (ATM) transfers; point-of-sale (POS) transfers; direct deposits or withdrawals of funds; transfers initiated by telephone; and transfers resulting from debit card transactions, whether or not initiated through an electronic terminal.

An automated teller machine (ATM) performs routine banking services using machines connected online to a bank computer system. Account holders are able to make deposits, transfer funds between accounts, and pay credit card statements and other bills

The advantages to using ATMs include:

- safer transactions, eliminating concerns for forged, counterfeit, altered, lost, or stolen checks;

- easy and convenient 24-hour access in many locations; and
- facilitation of online banking at a person's own bank.

For example, John Jones of the Jones Funeral home accepts cash payment from the family of Mary Smith for a $3,000 funeral service. He goes to his bank's ATM, places his debit card in the machine, inputs his PIN and – when requested by the ATM – submits the cash through the ATM for deposit into the funeral home account.

POS transfers use online terminals at retail outlets that allow a customer to transfer funds using their credit/debit cards to pay for goods or services. The procedure is similar to the use of an ATM. Using POS systems, consumers can carry less cash and take advantage of faster checkout times.

Using EFT direct deposits, customers have the ability to authorize a bank to allow another party – such as an employer or the government – to make direct deposits into their account. Similarly, a customer can grant permission for the bank to automatically make withdrawals for payments to another party – such as mortgage payments or paying for monthly streaming services.

Fees for using EFTs - A financial institution must disclose all fees for EFTs or the right to make EFTs. Unlike the required 'liabilities for unauthorized EFTs' disclosure, the act does not set any fee limitations; however a financial institution must disclose that networks used to complete the EFT – as well as an ATM operator – may charge a fee for an EFT or balance inquiries.

Chapter 12: Uniform Commercial Code Article 3 - Part 2

Overview
This chapter continues the review of Article 3 of the Uniform Commercial Code as it relates to negotiable instruments, also known as commercial paper. The chapter begins with a review of how negotiable instruments are transferred and thereafter examines endorsements, warranties, liabilities for payment, defenses for nonpayment, and holder in due course.

Chapter Definitions
Bearer paper - Negotiable instrument payable to bearer or cash.

Blank indorsement (endorsement) - having no words other than the signature of the endorser.

Consideration - the bargained-for exchange in a contract.

Draft - a written order by one person directing another to pay a sum of money, to a third person.

Drawee - the person, company or financial institution ordered to pay a draft.

Drawer - the person who executes any draft.

Endorsee (indorsee) - named holder of indorsed negotiable instrument.

Holder - one in possession of a negotiable instrument.

Indorsement (endorsement) - signature of holder on the back of a negotiable instrument, with any directions or limitations.

Indorser (endorser) - person who signs his or her name on back of an instrument.

Maker - the party who executes a promissory note.

Negotiation - the act of transferring ownership of a negotiable instrument to another party.

Note - a promise to pay money.

Order paper - Negotiable instrument made payable to the order of a named party; the word 'order' or its equivalent must be used.

Payee - the party to whom a negotiable instrument is made payable.

Promissory note - a negotiable instrument containing a promise to pay.

Qualified indorsement (endorsement) - an indorsement which limits the liability of the endorser.

Restrictive indorsement (endorsement) - indorsement that restricts use of a negotiable instrument.

Special indorsement (endorsement) - an indorsement which designates the particular person to whom payment is to be made.

Uniform Commercial Code (UCC) - model act that includes provisions concerning certain sales of goods and negotiable instruments.

Indorse or Endorse

For all practical purposes, there is no difference in the terms **indorse** and **endorse**, as they are simply two different spellings of the same word. **In**dorse is the common British spelling and **en**dorse is the common American spelling, similar to spellings for the color gr**a**y (American) and gr**e**y (British).

The reason for the disparity is the passage of time. When the Uniform Commercial Code (UCC) was created in 1896, indorse was the preferred spelling of that time period on both sides of the Atlantic. As a result, indorse and its derivatives were used all throughout the UCC. Now, 125 years later, indorse is usually only encountered in financial contexts and then only rarely. The common practice today is to use **en**dorse, as evidenced by virtually every banking institution printing 'endorsement' or 'endorse here' on the reverse side of checks to indicate where they must be signed.

For this chapter, the common spelling (endorse) and its derivatives as they are widely employed today in the United States are used.

Negotiable Instruments

West's Encyclopedia of American Law defines a negotiable instrument as:

> *A commercial paper, such as a check or promissory note, that contains the signature of the maker or drawer; an unconditional order or promise to pay a certain sum in cash that is payable either upon demand or at a specified designated time to the order of a designated person or to its bearer.*

Drafts and notes are the two categories of negotiable instruments (commercial paper). A **draft** is an *order* to pay money, and the person who executes a draft is a **drawer**. The most obvious examples of a draft would be personal checks and business checks.

A **note** is a *promise* to pay money, and the person who executes a note is a **maker**. An example of a note would be a student college loan. The student signs a note obligating them to repay the creditor – loan provider – the principal amount of the loan, in addition to any interest payments by a predetermined date.

Transfer of Negotiable Instruments

Negotiation - **Negotiation** is the act of transferring ownership of a negotiable instrument to another party. It involves a transfer to the extent the person to whom ownership is transferred becomes a **holder** of the instrument.

The required manner of negotiation (transfer) is determined by whether the instrument is an **order paper** (pay to the order of) or **bearer paper** (pay to bearer or cash). This is determined each time the instrument is transferred and may change back and forth between the two options several times.

When it comes to the manner of negotiation:

- an *order paper* is negotiated by the proper endorsement of the **payee** with delivery to the transferee. An endorsement must take place for negotiation to be complete. For example, if a check is delivered to a bank with no endorsement, there has been no negotiation.

- a *bearer paper* does not require an endorsement. The instrument itself is all that is needed to complete the negotiation. For example, a check made payable to 'Cash' is bearer paper, and any person that possesses the check is the holder of the instrument.

A further example: Bill Jones writes a check payable to Susan Smith. When Susan receives the check from Bill she is the holder of the negotiable instrument. If she wants to negotiate (transfer) the check to someone else, she must endorse the back of the check and deliver it to the other person. That other person then becomes the holder of the negotiable instrument.

Signatures - The UCC has an expansive view regarding what is a signature. They may be handwritten, typed, printed, marked (such as with an X), or a thumbprint. The instrument must be endorsed and the space for doing so this is usually on the reverse side. If space is needed for additional endorsements, a piece of paper – called an allonge when used for this purpose – may be securely attached to the instrument.

An endorser should sign their name exactly as it appears on the instrument. If the name is not spelled correctly, the payee can use the incorrect spelling, the correct spelling, or both. A misspelled name does not affect the negotiability of the instrument.

Holder - A holder is one in possession of commercial paper. The individual is either the original payee or has taken possession of the instrument thereafter by a valid negotiation with another.

For example, Bill Jones writes a check payable to Patty Payee. Upon receiving the check, Patty qualifies as the holder. If she wants to negotiate the check with another and thereby transfer the check to them, she must endorse the check and deliver it to the transferee. The transferee then qualifies as the holder.

Endorsements - An **endorsement** is the signature of a holder on the back of a negotiable instrument, together with any directions or limitations. The **endorsee** is the holder of an endorsed negotiable instrument, and the **endorser** is the person who signs their name on the back.

An endorsement may be used for the purposes of:

- negotiating the instrument,

- restricting payment of the instrument, or

➢ incurring an endorsers' liability on the instrument.

Forms of Endorsement

Special endorsement - This endorsement designates the person to whom payment is to be made. For example, Janet Jones endorses the back of a check by writing, 'Pay to Ben Smith,' and then signs her name. It is not necessary to use the words *order* or *bearer* in the endorsement. The instrument is still negotiable and can be negotiated further. The purpose in using a special endorsement is to prevent the check from being cashed by an unauthorized person.

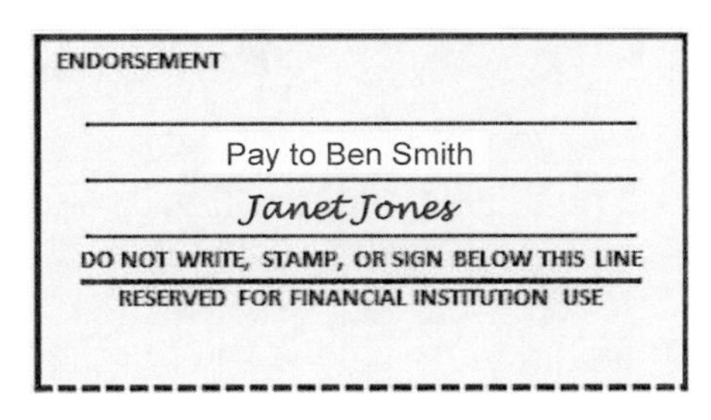

Blank endorsement - The name of this endorsement is a bit misleading, as the endorsement section on the reverse of the instrument is not entirely blank. It will contain the signature of the endorser but nothing else. For example, a check payable to the order of Janet Jones that she has endorsed on the reverse side with no additional instructions or limitations is a blank endorsement. When this occurs, the instrument becomes bearer paper, meaning anyone that possesses the instrument – such as a thief or finder – can negotiate it, including cashing it.

ENDORSEMENT
Janet Jones
DO NOT WRITE, STAMP, OR SIGN BELOW THIS LINE
RESERVED FOR FINANCIAL INSTITUTION USE

Restrictive endorsement - A restrictive indorsement is one which prevents the use of the instrument for anything except the stated use. For example, Bill Brown endorses the back of a check by writing restrictive language to state the check is presented for deposit only and then signs his name. In some cases, the restriction may include the account number to which the deposit should be made. A banking institution that receives a negotiable instrument with a restrictive endorsement must obey the restriction.

ENDORSEMENT
For Deposit Only
Bill Brown
DO NOT WRITE, STAMP, OR SIGN BELOW THIS LINE
RESERVED FOR FINANCIAL INSTITUTION USE

Qualified endorsement - This endorsement limits the liability of the endorser. The typical language used to express qualification is 'without recourse.' Endorsing a check and adding 'without recourse' serves to disclaim any liability of the subsequent holder of a financial instrument, i.e., the endorser takes no responsibility if the check bounces for insufficient funds. For example, if Bill Brown endorses a check by writing 'Pay to Pat Walsh without recourse' and then signs his name, he has disclaimed any liability to Pat Walsh. An instrument with this endorsement may still be negotiated further.

ENDORSEMENT
Pay to Pat Walsh, without recourse
Bill Brown
DO NOT WRITE, STAMP, OR SIGN BELOW THIS LINE
RESERVED FOR FINANCIAL INSTITUTION USE

Warranties

Unless specifically excluded, the person who transfers a negotiable instrument makes certain implied warranties. Warranty liability occurs even when a transferor does not endorse the instrument. There are two types of warranties: transfer and presentment.

Transfer warranties - The UCC provides an individual who transfers an instrument for **consideration** makes certain warranties to the transferee and – if the transfer is by endorsement – to all subsequent transferees and holders who take the instrument in good faith. These implied warranties include:

- the transferor is entitled to enforce the instrument;
- all signatures are authentic and authorized;
- the instrument has not been altered;
- the instrument is not subject to a claim or defense of any party which can be asserted against the transferor;
- the transferor has no knowledge of any insolvency (bankruptcy) proceedings against the maker, acceptor, or drawer; and
- with respect to a remotely-created consumer item, a bank that accepts and pays the instrument warrants to the next bank in the collection chain that the consumer authorized the item in that account.

Remotely-Created Consumer Items

A remotely-created consumer item is an item drawn on a consumer account that is not created by the payor bank. These items do not bear a handwritten signature purporting to be the signature of the drawer.

A bank that transfers or presents a remotely-created check would warrant the check is authorized by the person on whose account it is drawn. Generally – in place of a signature – a remotely created check bears a statement that the customer authorized the check or bears the customer's printed or typed name. Remotely-created checks can be useful payment devices. A debtor authorizing a credit card company to create a remotely created check by telephone enables the debtor to pay the credit card bill in a timely manner and avoid late charges.

Source: USLegal.com

Presentment warranties - An individual who presents an instrument for payment or acceptance makes the following implied warranties to any other person who in good faith pays or accepts the instrument.

- the person obtaining payment or acceptance is entitled to enforce the instrument or is authorized to obtain payment or acceptance on behalf of another person who is entitled to enforce the instrument;
- the instrument has not been altered;
- the person obtaining payment or acceptance has no knowledge that the signature of the issuer of the instrument is unauthorized; and

- regarding a remotely-created consumer item, that the person on whose account it is drawn authorized the issuance of the item in the amount that it was drawn.

Liability for Payment

Except for the endorser on a qualified endorsement, every party signing a negotiable instrument is either primarily or secondarily liable for payment on the instrument when it comes due.

Primary liability for payment - Only makers and acceptors are primarily liable for payment on a negotiable instrument and – unless there is a valid defense to payment – are absolutely required to pay the instrument. An acceptor is a **drawee** – the person, company, or financial institution expected to pay a check or draft when it is presented for payment. A maker is the party who executes a **promissory note** and by doing so unconditionally promises to pay the note. It is the maker's promise to pay that makes the note a negotiable instrument.

Secondary liability for payment - Secondary liability is attached when those who are primarily obligated to pay the holder fail to do so. Drawers and endorsers can be held secondarily liable to pay the instrument unless there is a valid defense to payment. Three conditions must be met before a party can be found liable.

1. The instrument must be properly and timely presented for payment. Presentment occurs when a person provides an instrument to either the party liable on the instrument for payment or to a drawee for acceptance. Under the UCC, a holder must present the instrument to the proper party in a timely fashion and if requested produce identification. The proper party for a note or certificate of deposit would be the maker. The proper party for a draft or check presented for payment would be the drawee. Presentment may be oral, in writing or by electronic media. Presentment is effective when the demand for payment or acceptance is received or if after a certain hour the next business day.

   Failure to present an instrument in a timely manner is the most common reason for improper presentment. Where a date has been provided for presentment, it must take place on that day. Such instruments must be presented for payment within a reasonable period of time after the party becomes liable for those instruments. The UCC specifies for drawers on uncertified checks, presentment must be made within 30 days following the date of the check or the date it was issued, whichever was later. With respect to endorsers, the UCC states presentment within seven days of endorsement is presumed to be reasonable. Presentment is not required when waived; cannot be made despite reasonable attempts; the maker, acceptor, or drawee has died or become insolvent; or the secondary party has no reason to expect the instrument will be paid.

2. The instrument must be dishonored. An instrument is dishonored when the required acceptance or payment is refused or cannot be obtained within the prescribed time. For example, the Smith Funeral Home handled the funeral for Paul Jones and the charges totaled $5000. Janet Jones, the widow, presented a personal check to the funeral home in that amount. The funeral home deposited the check, and a few days later the bank returned the check marked as unpaid due to 'insufficient funds,' an indication the account did not

have enough funds to cover the transaction. Jones personal check to the funeral home was therefore dishonored.

3. Notice of dishonor must be given to the party to be held liable. Once an instrument has been dishonored, proper notice must be given to those who have secondary liability. Notice may be given orally, in writing, or by email or other electronic media. Banks must give notice before midnight of the next banking day after receipt. Notice by any other party must be given within 30 days following the day of dishonor or the day on which the person who is liable receives notice of the dishonor.

Holder in Due Course (HDC)
From the Common Law to the UCC, there has been a strong policy to insulate remote or innocent purchasers of an instrument from disputes between the initial parties to the negotiable instrument. The individuals this policy is designed to protect are called a *holder in due course*.

As noted previously, a holder is one in possession of commercial paper. They are either the original payee or have taken possession of the instrument thereafter by a valid negotiation with another.

A person in possession of a negotiable instrument received in good faith without any notice of any defect in the instrument is a holder in due course and has greater enforcement rights than someone who is only a holder of a negotiable instrument.

West's Encyclopedia of American Law describes a holder in due course as:

> *An individual who takes a commercial paper for* ***value****, in* ***good faith****, with the belief that it is valid, with no knowledge of any defects.*
>
> *The UCC defines a holder in due course as one who takes an instrument for value in good faith absent any notice that it is* ***overdue****, has been dishonored, or is subject to any defense against it or claim to it by any other person.* [**Bold** emphasis added]

These are examples of how a party to a negotiable instrument becomes a holder in due course, which then affords them protections in the form of defenses to nonpayment.

Example 1: ***Value*** would exist when a holder negotiates (transfers) commercial paper to a CPA for services rendered.

Example 2: Phil issues a note to Louis who then negotiates the note to Dan. Dan is now a holder in due course, and if Phil were to raise a defense to payment, Dan would be protected if he did not know of the defense when he negotiated the note in ***good faith***.

Example 3: A note is due on April 1 but is negotiated to a holder in due course on May 1. This is an ***overdue*** (past due) note and will be dishonored if the maker refuses to pay the note. If the holder in due course is unaware of any dishonor at the time of negotiation, they would be protected from a defense to payment.

Note: A holder is not an innocent purchaser of a negotiable instrument if they know another person has a claim of ownership to the same instrument.

Shelter Rule

The shelter rule applies to an individual who does not qualify as a holder in due course but acquires the rights and privileges of a holder in due course.

The purpose of this rule is to allow a holder in due course – or whoever obtains those rights – to dispose of the instrument, thereby promoting the marketability and transferability of a negotiable instrument. Therefore, anyone – even those far removed from a holder in due course – can receive the rights of the holder in due course. A person cannot obtain these rights if a holder participated in a fraud or illegality regarding the instrument or had notice of a claim or defense on the instrument in question.

Personal (Limited) Defenses of Nonpayment

These types of defenses can be raised against an ordinary holder but not against holders in due course or those with the rights of a holder in due course.

Breach of contract or breach of warranty - When either of these conditions exist, the maker of the note can refuse to pay it, or the drawer of a check can stop payment.

Lack or failure of consideration - The lack of consideration – a bargained-for exchange in a contract – or failure to present consideration as agreed upon in a contract is a personal defense between the immediate parties to a negotiable instrument.

Fraud in the inducement (ordinary fraud) - This defense presents itself when a person is persuaded to sign an instrument based on the false statements of another. The person is fully aware they are signing a negotiable instrument but not aware the other party has misrepresented a material fact.

For example, Frank bought a used car from Sam after being told by Sam he had put a new transmission in the car. Frank relied on Sam's statement and signed a $3000 promissory note to pay for the car. In truth, Sam did not replace the transmission, and a week after buying the car Frank was told he needed a new transmission. Frank can use this act of fraud as a defense to nonpayment of the promissory note.

Payment or partial payment - A party who pays a negotiable instrument should demand a surrender of the instrument itself. If the instrument is not surrendered, it may be subject to further negotiation by the holder to another party – whether by accident or deliberately – who may then demand payment of the same instrument again. When making a partial payment, the payer should ensure the partial payment is noted on the instrument so any other person taking the instrument will have notice.

For example, Jim borrows $500 from Alex to make a down payment on a used car and gives Alex a thirty-day promissory note. Within fifteen days, Jim pays off the note but does not ask Alex to return the note. If Alex negotiates the note to Fred before the thirty days has passed, Fred becomes a holder in due course and Jim will have to pay the note again to Fred.

Non-delivery - Delivery of an instrument to an innocent purchaser without the permission of the maker is a personal defense.

For example, Ann makes out a check payable to cash and leaves it on her desk at home. Her home is burglarized by Ken who takes the check and negotiates it to John, who becomes a holder in due course. John can collect the amount of the check from Ann but Ken cannot collect from Ann.

Theft - Someone who steals a negotiable instrument may qualify as holder of the instrument. However, the payor may assert a defense against payment to the holder based on the theft.

Improper completion - There are times when a signed but incomplete instrument may be transferred to another person.

For example, Alan made out a promissory note but did not name the payee. He then signed it and promptly lost it. Billy finds the note, fills his name in as the payee, and negotiates the note to Paul who then becomes a holder in due course. Although Billy cannot collect from Alan, Paul can collect from Alan.

Real (Universal) Defenses of Nonpayment

These types of defenses can be raised against all holders including a holder in due course and those who possess an instrument through a holder in due course.

Forgery of a signature - A forged signature cannot be used to bind the person whose name is listed as the payee on the instrument, unless that person approves of the signature or is stopped from denying it because the forgery was made possible through the negligence of the maker or drawer.

Fraud in the execution - This exists when one party obtains a negotiable instrument through fraud or trickery, and there was no intention to create a negotiable instrument.

For example, Fred – 89 years old – signs a form thinking it is a request for credit. In reality, Jim defrauded Fred to get him to sign a promissory note. Fred cannot be made to pay on the promissory note due to Jim's fraudulent actions.

Discharge in bankruptcy - A discharge in bankruptcy provides an immediate defense to any nonpayment of a negotiable instrument associated with the bankruptcy.

Infancy (minority) - Infancy is considered a real defense necessary to protect infants from adults who are in the position to take advantage of them through contractual dealings.

Hybrid Defenses

Certain defenses can be personal or real depending on the factual situation.

Illegality - It is a real defense in those cases where the law holds an instrument is *void* because it was issued regarding illegal conduct. However, where the law declares an instrument is *voidable* due to illegality, it becomes a personal defense.

Mental incapacity - If a court declares an individual who signed a negotiable instrument is mentally incompetent, their action is subject to a real defense. However, if the law holds an instrument is *voidable* due to mental incapacity, then it is a personal defense.

Duress - If the law states an instrument is voidable due to *ordinary* duress, the defense is personal. Ordinary or slight duress exists when there are threats that prevent someone from exercising free will. That person will not be held liable on the instrument to the individual who actually committed the duress. However, if the individual signs an instrument under immediate threat of force or violence, that would be considered *extreme* duress and a real defense.

Alteration - An unauthorized change to an important element in a negotiable instrument or contract that affects the rights of the parties is an alteration. When this occurs, the maker or drawer of an instrument is obligated to pay according to the original terms not the altered terms. Examples of alterations include changing the place or date of the instrument or adding or changing an interest rate. An alteration can be enforced by a holder according to its original unaltered terms or to its terms as completed.

Chapter 13: Employment Law

Overview
This chapter explores employer/employee relationships and employer/independent contractor relationships in the workplace, with an emphasis on those that take place in the funeral service industry. The chapter concludes with information on discrimination in employment and protections afforded to employees.

Chapter Definitions
Employee - A person hired to perform work that is directed and controlled by the employer.

Employer - The party who employs employees to do certain work.

Independent contractor - One who contracts to do jobs and is controlled only by the contract as to how performance is to be rendered.

Salary - Generally considered to be compensation for managerial or administrative services expressed in terms of a month or year.

W-2 form - Wage and tax statement; a report furnished by the employer for each employee indicating gross earnings and deductions.

Wage - A form of compensation usually for skilled and unskilled labor expressed in terms of hours, weeks or pieces completed.

Employer-Employee Relationships
An employment relationship can be seen as a voluntary arrangement between an **employer** – who hires an employee to do certain work; and an **employee** – the person hired to perform the work as directed and controlled by the employer. An **independent contractor** may also be employed by an employer but is not controlled as to how to perform the work to be performed.

Employee rights and benefits may depend on whether they are employed in a full-time or part-part capacity. Generally, employers define a full-time employee as someone who works between 35 and 40 hours in a seven-day workweek.

An employee can be compensated through a **salary** which is generally considered to be compensation for managerial or administrative services expressed in terms of a month or year. An employee may be compensated by a **wage** – a form of compensation usually for skilled and unskilled labor expressed in terms of hours, weeks, or pieces completed.

Employment-at-Will
Historically, employers have held a great deal of authority on who they can hire and terminate as an employee. The common law doctrine of employment-at-will was the means by which both employers and employees dealt with employment situations. This doctrine provides for an employer to terminate an employee at any time for any reason, and an employee to terminate their employment at any time for any reason. This doctrine is applied in every state but Montana. While

this doctrine is still in use, it has been eroded and modified by the states and courts providing a number of exceptions that require an employer demonstrate an employee termination is justified. There are five discharge exceptions that have been recognized.

1. *Discharge in violation of the law* - There are certain laws that prohibit firing an employee at will, including the Civil Rights Act that prevents a discharge due to race, color, religion, sex, or national origin. In addition, the Occupational Safety and Health Act prevents an employee from being fired for complaining that an employer has violated the health and safety requirements of the Act; and the Fair Labor Standards Act prohibits firing an employee who complains an employer has violated wage and hour provisions of the Act.

2. *Discharge in violation of established public policy* - Many states have enacted whistleblower laws that prevent an employer from terminating an employee when they file a workers' compensation claim or complain the employer violated a labor law. Additionally, most states prohibit an employer from firing an employee who refuses to do something illegal or violates public policy.

3. *Discharge prohibited based on implied contract terms* - Implied contract terms may be created through oral assurances by a supervisor; or employers' handbooks, policies, practices, or other written assurances. Courts may review whether these employment policies were in existence when the employee was hired; whether or not the employee knew about the policies; and if the employer had the right to change the policies at any time. Ultimately, a court may then hold the language used in implied contract terms prohibits a discharge.

4. *Discharge prohibited because of wrongful employer acts (torts)* - A few courts have prohibited a firing based on the at-will doctrine if the employee can substantiate an abusive discharge procedure was used by the employer, which may then result in a lawsuit for intentional infliction of emotional distress, defamation, or fraud.

5. *Discharge prohibited if not done in good faith* - A minority of states prohibit the termination of any employee if not done in good faith. Courts have required just cause for termination and will not allow them when made in bad faith or caused by malice on the part of the employer.

Employment Contracts and Union Contracts

Employment contracts - These contracts can be in writing or oral, and the relationships can exist for a fixed and definite period of time or may be terminated for cause or under specified conditions. If a contract is for a time period of more than one year, it must be in writing to satisfy the Statute of Frauds. Employment contracts frequently have clauses regarding confidentiality in relation to trade secrets, restrictive covenants, compensation arrangements, bonuses and other fringe benefits, and an agreement to arbitration if there is a dispute between the parties.

Union contracts - Collective bargaining between an employer and a large number of employees has become common practice as unions negotiate employment contracts. The union acts as the agent of the employees and bargains for wages, hours, rights, and benefits, as well as the length of the contract. Once an agreement is negotiated and tentatively approved by the employer and union negotiators, the full union membership votes on whether or not to accept the contract. If approved, the contract between the employer and the union representing the employees is called a collective bargaining agreement.

Duties and Liabilities of an Employer

Duty to exercise care - Employers must act as a reasonable person would to avoid harm to an employee.

Duty to provide a reasonably safe place to work - This duty has been codified in OSHA requirements. What constitutes a safe place to work depends on the type of work involved.

Duty to provide safe tools and appliances - Any equipment provided to an employee to perform their job must be safe for use. This also applies to machinery.

Duty to provide competent and sufficient employees for the task - An employer could be found liable for injuries to employees caused by an insufficient number of workers or the lack of skills thereof.

Duty to instruct employees - The employer has a specific duty to instruct an employee in the use and handling of machinery, chemicals, and electrical appliances that are used in the workplace environment.

Employee Duties to the Employer

Job performance - An employee is required to perform the job duties to the best of their ability and to advance the employers interests.

Business confidentiality - An employee has the duty to maintain confidential business matters including trade secrets and other matters that remain confidential to the business concerned.

Inventions - Unless there is an agreement between the employee and the employer, any inventions created by the employee belong to the employee. If an invention is developed during working hours while using the employer's resources, an employer has a 'shop rite' to use the invention without charge in the employer's business.

Statutory Modifications of Common Law

Workers' compensation - States have enacted laws allowing injured workers and their survivors to be compensated if injuries or death occur in the scope of their employment. Employees are entitled to benefits even if the employer is not negligent and/or the employee is negligent. Injured employees may also sue third parties who may be negligently responsible for their injuries.

Unemployment compensation - The *Federal Unemployment Tax Act* requires employers to contribute to financing the administrative costs of federal and state unemployment compensation programs. Individual states set the eligibility requirements for unemployment programs and the federal government cooperates with the states in furnishing unemployment compensation to eligible individuals. The states make payments to the unemployed worker while the federal government pays the cost of running the program.

At a minimum, to be eligible for unemployment benefits a person must be ready, available, and able to work and not refuse any appropriate employment opportunity. Individuals who are self-employed, on strike, or who voluntarily quit a job without cause are ineligible for benefits.

Occupational Safety and Health Administration (OSHA) - OSHA is responsible for regulation and enforcement of safety and health matters for most employees. OSHA requires employers to provide a safe and healthy workplace for employees and to do so through training programs and making safety information readily available in the workplace. There are a number of standards developed by OSHA that are applicable to the funeral service industry, including the Formaldehyde Exposure; Hazard Communication; Bloodborne Pathogen; and Personal Protective Equipment standards.

Immigration Reform Act - This federal legislation requires employers to check the immigration status of applicants to ensure they are either U.S. citizens or documented noncitizens authorized to work in the United States.

Employer Liability

Vicarious liability - Cornell Law School Legal Information Institute defines vicarious liability as:

> *Liability that a supervisory party (such as an employer) bears for the actionable conduct of a subordinate or associate (such as an employee) based on the relationship between the two parties.*

As a matter of public policy, courts have held employers are vicariously liable for injuries or property damage caused by their employees when acting within the scope of their employment. This doctrine is known as 'respondeat superior,' a Latin term meaning 'let the master respond.'

For example, Eddie Jones is a funeral director at the Davis Funeral Home and his supervisor sends him to make a removal. Eddie, driving the funeral home hearse, makes an illegal left turn in front of another car and causes an accident. Because Eddie was acting in the scope of his employment as a funeral director and furthering the business of his employer, the Davis Funeral Home may be held liable to the driver of the other vehicle. If an employee causes an injury or damage to a third party that was not a part or result of their employment, the employer would have no liability for the actions of the employee, but the employee could be exposed to a potential civil tort claim.

Direct liability - An employer can be held directly liable for injury or damages caused by an employee under any of these circumstances:

- the employer ordered the act that caused the injury;
- the employer had knowledge of the act in question and allowed it to occur;
- employer negligence in not enforcing a safe working environment; or
- an employer not providing safe equipment, tools, and machinery in the workplace.

In addition – under the doctrine of negligent employment – employers have a duty to investigate the background of an applicant. If it can be shown the employer failed to exercise due diligence in conducting the inquiry or hired an incompetent worker, they may be directly liable for the actions of that worker if they cause an injury or damages. If after hiring the worker the employer learns of a problem or dangerous tendencies of the employee – and fails to take action – they could be found liable under the negligent employment doctrine.

Employee vs. Independent Contractor

Employee - An employee is the person hired to perform work as directed and controlled by an employer. The employee performs the work while under the control and supervision of the employer as to the work to be performed and the manner in which it is to be completed.

Independent contractor - An independent contractor is one who contracts to do jobs for another and is controlled only by the contract as to how the performance (work) is to be rendered. In essence, the independent contractor performs certain tasks for a set fee but is not subject to the control of the contracting party as to how the job is to be carried out. Independent contractors include such persons as freelance writers, plumbers, or photographers. Generally, an independent contractor cannot impose vicarious liability on the employer.

It is important to recognize the differences between an employer/employee relationship and an independent contractor relationship can impact whether employee benefits and payroll taxes apply. If a dispute arises, courts will seek to determine if a person performing services for another is an employee or independent contractor. The court may seek answers to these questions:

- How much control does the employer have over the details of the work? If the employer exercises control over the methods of getting the work completed, a court would likely view the individual as an employee.

- Is the worker in an occupation or business distinct from that of the employer? If they are it would point to an independent contractor status.

- Is the work done being performed under the direction of the employer, or by a specialist without supervision? If performed under an employer's direction, the worker would be an employee; if by a specialist without supervision, an independent contractor.

- Does the employer supply the tools at the place of work? If they do it is an indication the worker is an employee.

- For how long has the worker been employed? If for a long period of time, this would indicate the worker is an employee.

- Is the worker providing services for a set time period, such as weekly or biweekly; or by the job with no time parameters? Payment by the job is a strong indication of an independent contractor relationship.

- ➢ What degree of skill is required and who trained the worker? If little skill is needed, or the worker is trained by the one who hired them, this would be a sign of an employer/employee relationship.

Income tax requirements - The Internal Revenue Service (IRS) publishes criteria to aid employers in determining whether a worker is an employee or independent contractor, and recognizes to determine such status depends on the facts of each situation. Income records and reporting requirements for employees and independent contractors are not the same.

For income tax purposes, the earnings of an *employee* are subject to income tax withholding and the employer is required to withhold and remit those taxes to the applicable federal and state tax agencies. The employer is also responsible for providing each employee with a W-2 wage and tax statement (**W-2 form**) that provides gross earnings and income tax deductions for a calendar year.

For an *independent contractor*, the employer is not required to withhold or remit any income taxes but must provide the contractor with a 1099 Miscellaneous Income statement. A copy of this statement must also be sent to applicable tax agencies. The contractor is responsible for paying any income taxes that are due directly to tax authorities.

If the IRS learns a company or employer has misclassified an individual as an independent contractor, the employer may be required to pay any applicable withholding and employment taxes, as well as be assessed substantial penalties for non-compliance with income tax laws.

<u>Discrimination in Employment</u>
Civil Rights Act of 1964 (Title VII) - This act prohibits discrimination on the basis of race, color, religion, sex, or national origin. Other significant features include the prohibition of job discrimination and the creation of the Equal Employment Opportunities Commission (EEOC). The Act applies to all employers having 15 or more employees.

Title VII forbids discrimination in any aspect of employment, including:

Hiring and firing	Job advertisements	Use of company facilities
Assignment or classification of employees	Training and apprenticeship programs	Any other terms and conditions of employment
Recruitment	Testing	Fringe benefits
Transfer, promotion, layoff, or recall	Pay, retirement plans and disability leave	Compensation of employees

Fair Labor Standards Act (FSLA) - This act establishes minimum wage, overtime pay, recordkeeping, and child labor standards affecting full-time and part-time workers in the private sector. It is enforced by the Wage and Hour Division of the U.S. Department of Labor. The FSLA has jurisdiction over funeral establishments if they have gross annual sales that exceed $500,000. At the time of this writing, the federal minimum wage is $7.25 per hour. Each state is free to set its own minimum wage or not have a minimum.

The equal pay provisions of the FLSA prohibit sex-based wage differentials between men and women employed in the same establishment who perform jobs that require equal skill, effort, and responsibility and which are performed under similar working conditions. This act also applies to all employment positions, including any members of an exempt class; however, unequal pay may be acceptable if appointments or promotions are based on a seniority or merit-based system.

Age Discrimination in Employment Act (ADEA) - This act protects certain applicants and employees 40 years of age and older from discrimination on the basis of age in hiring, promotion, discharge, compensation, or terms, conditions, and privileges of employment. Age discrimination involves treating an applicant or employee less favorably because of his or her age. The Act applies to all employers having 20 or more employees. The administration and enforcement of the ADEA falls under the jurisdiction of the EEOC.

Americans with Disabilities Act (ADA) - This act prohibits discrimination against the disabled in employment, public transportation, telecommunication services, and public accommodations and services. The review here focuses on the ADA as it relates to *employment.* The ADA prohibits funeral establishments with 15 or more employees from discriminating against qualified individuals with disabilities in job application procedures, hiring, firing, advancement, compensation, job training, and other terms, conditions, and privileges of employment.

An individual with a disability is a person who:

- has a physical or mental impairment that substantially limits one or more major life activities;
- has a record of such an impairment; or
- is regarded as having such an impairment.

A qualified employee or applicant with a disability is an individual who – with or without a reasonable accommodation – can perform the essential functions of the job. An employer is required to make a reasonable accommodation to the known disability of a qualified applicant or employee if it would not impose an undue hardship on the operation of the employers' business.

Reasonable accommodations are adjustments or modifications provided by an employer to enable people with disabilities to enjoy equal employment opportunities. Accommodations vary depending on the needs of the individual employee, and not all people with disabilities – or even all people with the same disability – require the same accommodation. Reasonable accommodations may include such things as:

Making existing facilities accessible	Job restructuring
Part-time or modified work schedules	Acquiring or modifying equipment
Changing tests, training materials, or policies	Reassignment to a vacant position
Providing qualified readers or interpreters	

Protections for Employees

Family and Medical Leave Act (FMLA) - This act entitles eligible employees of covered employers to take unpaid, job-protected leave for specified family and medical reasons. While on leave, the employer must continue their group health insurance coverage under the same terms and conditions as if the employee had not taken leave. The FMLA applies to employers that have 50 or more employees in 20 or more workweeks in the current or preceding calendar year. Only eligible employees are entitled to take FMLA leave.

An eligible employee is one who:

- works for a covered employer;
- has worked for the employer for at least 12 months;
- has at least 1,250 hours of service for the employer during the 12-month period immediately preceding the leave; and
- works at a location where the employer has at least 50 employees within 75 miles.

When an employee is ready to return to work, the employer must give them the same position held at the time of leave. If this is not possible, the employer must place the employee in an equivalent position in terms of pay, benefits or other terms or conditions of employment.

Patient Protection and Affordable Care Act - This act increased health insurance coverage for the uninsured and implemented reforms to the health insurance market. Sometimes referred to as Obamacare, this legislation requires employers with 50 or more employees to provide employee health insurance.

Health Insurance Portability and Accountability Act (HIPPA) - This act – known informally as the Privacy Rule – establishes national standards to protect an individual's medical records and other personal health information. The Act requires appropriate safeguards to protect the privacy of this data and sets forth limits and conditions on the acceptable uses and disclosures that may be made without patient authorization. HIPPA strictly limits an employer's ability to exclude coverage for pre-existing conditions other than for pregnancy.

Chapter 14: Agency Relationships

Overview

A contract with third parties on behalf of a principal is what distinguishes an agency relationship from other employment relationships. This chapter explores the creation of an agency relationship; duties to and from a principal, agent and third party; and termination of such relationships.

Chapter Definitions

Agent - The party appointed by the principal to enter into a contract with a third party on behalf of the principal.

Apparent authority - The authority an agent is believed by third parties to have because of the principal's behavior.

Authority - The power to act for someone else.

Durable power of attorney - A power of attorney that remains in effect after the disability or incapacity of the principal.

Express authority - Authority of an agent, stated in the agreement creating the agency.

Fiduciary - a person in a relationship of trust and confidence.

General agent - One who is given broad authority to conduct the principal's business.

General Power of Attorney - A written instrument granting the agent broad powers to act for the principal.

Implied authority - An agent's authority to do things in order to carry out express authority.

Indemnification - a legal agreement by one party to hold another party not liable for potential losses or damages.

Power of attorney - An instrument granting someone authority to act as agent or attorney-in-fact for the principal; an ordinary power of attorney is revocable and automatically terminates upon the death or incapacity of the principal.

Principal - A party who appoints another to serve as an agent.

Special Agent - One authorized by the principal to execute specific act(s).

Springing power of attorney - A written instrument authorizing one person to act as an agent for another effective only upon a certain event occurring.

Statute of Frauds - law requiring certain contracts be in writing to be enforceable.

Agency Relationships

An agency relationship exists when one person (the **principal**) reaches an agreement with another person (the **agent**) who agrees to act on the principal's behalf and under the principal's control. The agency relationship is that of a **fiduciary**, defined as a person in a relationship of trust and confidence. Given the complexities in business and the world, an agency is vitally important to ensure transactions between parties can be completed properly.

When an agent negotiates a contract or agreement there are at least three parties: (1) the *principal*, the party who appoints another to serve as an agent; (2) the *agent*, the party appointed by the principal to enter into a contract or agreement on their behalf with a (3) *third party*. Principals, agents, and third parties may be individuals, partnerships, or corporations.

Agency Documents

The document creating an agency may be called a **power of attorney** – an instrument granting someone authority to act as an agent (called an attorney-in-fact) for the principal. Agency relationships may be called agreements, contracts, or other similar terms.

There are three common power of attorney types funeral directors should be familiar with.

1. A **general power of attorney** is a written instrument granting an agent broad powers to act for the principal. They may be called an *ordinary* power of attorney. This type of POA ceases to exist upon the disability or incapacity of the principal.

2. A **springing power of attorney** is a written instrument authorizing one person to act as an agent for another, effective only upon a certain event occurring (springing). They are commonly employed by individuals that wish to delegate an agent to manage their affairs in the event they become disabled or mentally incompetent. They typically will require a medical doctor or mental health professional to attest to any disability or mental condition when the delegated agent believes they should start making decisions for the principal. They may also be called a *conditional* power of attorney.

3. A **durable power of attorney** provides the authority granted under a power of attorney will remain in effect even after the disability or incapacity of the principal.

A person with authority over the affairs of another by means of any type of a Power of Attorney ceases to have such authority once the person they represent dies.

The three most common power of attorney types described above are found in the majority of the states, but some may use a slightly different name based on the authority granted to the agent.

For example, some states recognize:

- a medical power of attorney to grant authority to act in matters of health and well-being;

- a limited power of attorney for a very specific purpose, such as signing a legal document when the principal is not available to do so for themselves; or

- a financial power of attorney with respect to fiscal and monetary matters.

In virtually all cases, the addition of the word 'durable' to the name of a power of attorney type extends the power being granted to remain in effect even after the disability or incapacity of the principal.

The statutes on the use of a power of attorney to delegate authority to an Agent are not consistent across the 50 states, although the differences are usually not significant. Regardless, funeral directors must be familiar with the laws pertaining to these very powerful documents in the states where they practice.

Creating an Agency Relationship

The creation of an agency relationship may be accomplished by:

- agreement.
- ratification,
- necessity, or
- operation of law.

By agreement - By agreement is the most common way of creating an agency, and the agreement usually states the rights and duties of both the principal and agent; the agency relationship duration; and other conditions as agreed upon by the parties. While an agency contract may be oral or written, the requirements of the **Statute of Frauds** – which requires certain contracts be in writing to be enforceable – may apply to some agency relationships.

By ratification - Ratification of an agency relationship occurs when the principal *approves* by word or action – express or implied – an *unauthorized act* undertaken by an agent, or approves an act done in the principal's name by an *unauthorized individual*. The agent acts on behalf of an identified principal who *later* ratifies the action. The principal must know all the material facts involved in the agreement or contract. If they ratify the agreement and later find they did not know all the material facts at that time, they can cancel the contract.

By necessity - An agency relationship may be created when circumstances make it necessary. For example, there are some states that allow the creation of an agency relationship when a person fails to support their spouse or minor children.

By operation of law - This agency relationship can be created when a court determines a certain social policy needs to be achieved

For example, this could exist in a family situation where parents may not be providing for the basic necessities of their children – essentials necessary for a person to live a healthy and comfortable life. In this situation, a court could appoint an agent – called a guardian ad litem – with the power to provide for the child.

An agency may also be created by estoppel. Will Kenton, in an article on the Investopedia website, defines estoppel as:

> *... a legal principle that prevents someone from arguing something or asserting a right that contradicts what they previously said or agreed to by law. It is meant to prevent people from being unjustly wronged by the inconsistencies of another person's words or actions.*

With respect to agency relationships, when a principal causes a third party to believe that another person has the authority to act as the principal's agent, the principal is estopped from denying the agency relationship exits. Here, the principal has created the appearance of an agency which does not exist. To be successful in court, the third party must prove they reasonably believed the principal's actions demonstrated an agency relationship did exist.

Authority of an Agent

An agent has the **authority** and power to act for someone else, and a principal can delegate to an agent the same powers they themselves possess. There are no qualifications or legal requirements to serve as an agent, except in those cases where a state or local law may require a person to be licensed or registered to perform a certain task, such as a real estate broker. Any legally competent person can appoint and act through an agent. In fact a minor can appoint an agent, but the appointment may be voidable or void dependent on the laws of the state in which the agency relationship was established.

Express authority (authority by appointment) - **Express authority** is the authority of an agent stated in the agreement or contract that created the agency relationship. It can be oral or written. In those cases where it must be in writing, the Equal Dignity Rule provides the agent's authority must also be in writing. The Rule is a legal doctrine stipulating that when a contract must be in writing, then the authority for an agent to enter into such a contract must also be in writing. For example, if a contract must be in writing in order to satisfy the Statute of Frauds, then the authority of an agent to enter into such a contract on behalf of a principal must also be in writing.

Implied authority - **Implied authority** is an agent's authority to do things in order to carry out express authority. It enables the agent to perform acts reasonably necessary to accomplish the purposes of the agency relationship. This authority can also be implied by custom or inferred from the position the agent holds.

For example, Frank is employed by Smith's Supermarket as the store manager but does not have the authority to contract with third parties. Nonetheless, the duty of managing a supermarket implies the authority to do what is reasonably necessary to run the store. This can include the hiring of employees, purchasing merchandise for resale, and publishing advertisements for special store sales.

Apparent authority - **Apparent authority** is the authority third parties believe an agent has because of the principal's behavior. For this to exist, there must be a reasonable belief on the part of the third party. Apparent authority generally evolves through a principal's pattern of conduct over a period of time.

Liability - A principal is liable for an agents torts and crimes that occur at the direction of the principal, or when the agent is performing duties in the ordinary course of the agency agreement. An agent acting at the principal's direction may also be held liable for a tort even if they did not know the tortious act was wrong. Regardless, an agent is always liable for his or her torts.

Classification of Agents

General agents are those who are given broad authority to conduct the principal's business. For example, Jerry Jones is the manager of the Smith Funeral Home and enters into an agency agreement with Joe Smith, the owner of the funeral home. As an agent, Jerry has the authority to buy and sell merchandise, hire and fire employees, and pay the bills from the business accounts of the funeral home.

Special agents are those authorized by the principal to execute specific acts. A real estate broker is one example of a special agent. Another example is a *factor or commission merchant*. This is a person who receives possession of another's property to sell on commission. The merchant typically sells in their own name, although they can sell in the name of the principal. When a commission merchant agent sells the property, they deduct their fee and remit the remainder to the principal.

Duties of the Agent to the Principal

Loyalty and good faith - An agent must work solely for the benefit of the principal and not for the agent or a third party. This is a part of the fiduciary relationship that exists between the parties.

Obedience - The agent must follow all lawful and clearly stated instructions from the principal. Any deviation from those directions is a violation of the agents duties. If the instructions to the agent are not clear, they must still act in good faith and in a manner reasonable under the circumstances. In an emergency – if the principal cannot be consulted – the agent may deviate from the instructions without violating their duty.

Reasonable skill and diligence - An implied condition of an agency relationship is that the agent will use reasonable diligence and skill performing their duties. The standard of care is that which a reasonable person would exercise under similar circumstances. Any failure of performance can lead to an action for a breach of contract.

Accounting - The agent is responsible for keeping – and making available to the principal – an account of all property and funds received by or disbursed to others on behalf of the principal. In addition, the agent has a duty to maintain separate financial accounts for the funds that belong to the principal and the personal funds of the agent. Commingling of these funds in not permitted or acceptable.

Information - The agent is required to notify the principal of all matters that come to their attention regarding the purposes or transactions of the agency relationship. A notice from others to the agent is considered a notice to the principal and that information must be passed on..

Duties of the Principal to the Agent

Compensation - A principal must pay the agent compensation as provided for in the agency agreement. If not provided in the agreement, compensation must be reasonable and customary. If there is a contingency agreement for payment, the agent is only paid when the contingency has been met.

Reimbursement - The principal is obligated to reimburse the agent for any expenses the agent paid from their own personal funds.

Indemnification - It is common practice in business matters and contractual agreements for documentation to include an **indemnification** clause to protect (indemnify) the parties from certain liabilities.

Black's Law Dictionary defines indemnify as meaning:

> *To save harmless; to secure against loss or damage; to give security for the reimbursement of a person in case of an anticipated loss falling upon him. Also, to make good; to compensate; to make reimbursement to one of a loss already incurred by him.*

Subject to the agency agreement, a principal has a duty to pay or indemnify (hold harmless) the agent for any liabilities due to authorized and lawful acts.

Adherence to contract terms - A principal must comply with the terms of contracts made by the agent in their name and fully cooperate with the agent so agency duties can be completed.

Duties of Principals and Agents to Third Parties

Principals - A principal is responsible to a third party for all agreements made by the agent on behalf of the principal within the scope of their agency. The principal is not liable to a third party if they did not authorize the agreement made by the agent and the agent acted outside the scope of their agency.

Agents - If the principal's identity is known (disclosed) to a third party at the time a contract is made with the agent, the agent cannot be held responsible for the contract as long as the agent acts within the scope of their actual authority.

If the principal's identity is not known (undisclosed) to a third party and they do not know the agent is acting for a principal, the agent can be held liable for their actions. The correct way for an agent to sign and bind only the principal is to sign as: '*principal, by agent.*

A partially disclosed principal situation exists when an agent tells a third party they are acting on behalf of someone else but do not know the identity of the principal. In these cases, the agent can be held liable.

In all cases, an agent will be held personally liable for fraud or any other illegality caused by their carelessness, disobedience, or malice committed on the order of the principal.

<u>Termination by Act of the Parties</u>
Original agreement - If there is a date certain for the agency relationship to end, it automatically terminates on that date. If a special agent has completed a stated task in the agreement – such as selling an automobile – then the agency ends when the car is sold.

Subsequent agreement - A principal and an agent can agree to end the agency relationship at any time.

Renunciation - An agent has the power to renounce the agency at any time; however, if the agent abandons the agency without just cause, they can be held liable for any loss or damages incurred by the principal.

Revocation - Generally speaking, a principal can revoke the authority of any agent with or without cause at any time. The principal can give notice of the revocation directly to the agent or take actions that would be inconsistent with continuing the agency. A revocation is considered a discharge.

There is a difference between the right to revoke the agency agreement and having the power to do so. If the discharge is for a good reason – such as failure to follow directions – the agent may not recover any damages for a breach of contract. In fact, the agent may be required to pay monetary damages to the principal for causing the breach. However, if the agent is wrongfully discharged, the agent may collect unpaid compensation up to the time of their discharge, along with any potential losses or damages that occur as a result of the wrongful discharge.

A principal cannot unilaterally revoke the authority of any agent if the agent has a personal interest in the agency. The interest in this situation is called an '*agency coupled with an interest*.' The interest may be in the form of an interest in the authority or an interest in the subject matter.

Examples:
An *interest in the authority* would exist when the principal and agent agree the agent will collect money from another person, except the agent then keeps the money received for a pre-existing debt with the principal.

An *interest in the subject matter* would exist when the agent has possession or control over the real property of the principal and also has other legal rights in the same property.

<u>Termination by Operation of Law</u>
Subsequent illegality of subject matter - The relationship between the principal and the agent end if the subject matter of the agreement becomes illegal.

Death or incapacity of either party - The death or incapacity of either the principal or agent terminates the agency relationship, except when incapacity is the issue and the principal has a durable power of attorney agreement.

Destruction of subject matter - For example, the accidental destruction of a motor vehicle that was to be sold by an agent for the principal would terminate the agency relationship.

Bankruptcy of principal - The bankruptcy of the principal immediately terminates the agency relationship, but in most cases the bankruptcy of the agent would not terminate the relationship.

Dissolution of corporation - A dissolution of a corporation is the termination of all corporate operations, including any agency agreements or relationships.

War - If the principal and agent live in countries that are at war with one another, the agent's authority is terminated or in some cases may lapse until peace is achieved.

A principal must give third parties who have dealt with the agent notice of an agency termination. If they do not give notice, they could be bound by actions of the agent that occur after the agency was terminated and the third parties were unaware. Notices to any third parties should be in writing, but notice is not required if an agency is terminated by an operation of law.

Chapter 15: Non-Corporation Business Organizations

Overview

There are several different business organization models under which a new funeral establishment may be formed. These models may be categorized as being either a non-corporation type of business structure or a corporation type of business structure. This chapter explores the non-corporation types, including sole proprietorships, partnerships, and limited liability companies.

Chapter Definitions

Breach of contract - failure or refusal to perform contractual obligations.

Contract - a legally enforceable agreement.

Dissolution - in business matters, the official act or process of formally ending the operations of an enterprise, such as a corporation [by Author].

General partner - individual actively and openly engaged in the business and held to everyone as a partner.

Liability - responsibility for actions and/or other debts; the quality or state of being legally obligated or accountable.

Limited liability company (LLC) - hybrid form of business organization that combines features of both a corporation and partnership.

Limited partner - partner whose liability for the firm's debts is limited to the amount of his or her investment.

Partnership - the voluntary association of two or more people who have combined their resources to carry on as co-owners a lawful enterprise for their joint profit.

Silent partner - an individual who takes no active part in the management of a partnership, but has capital invested in the business.

Sole proprietorship - a business owned by one person, who is personally subject to claims of creditors.

Tort - a private or civil wrong against a person or his or her property, other than by breach of contract, for which there may be action for damages.

Business Organization Models

A funeral director planning to open and operate a funeral establishment needs to consider the types of business organization models available to them in their home state. Only by the close examination of the pros and cons for each will they be in a position to determine the type most advantageous to their goals and objectives for the business they envision. The chart that follows illustrates the types of business organization models that are reviewed in this chapter and those that are reviewed in the next chapter.

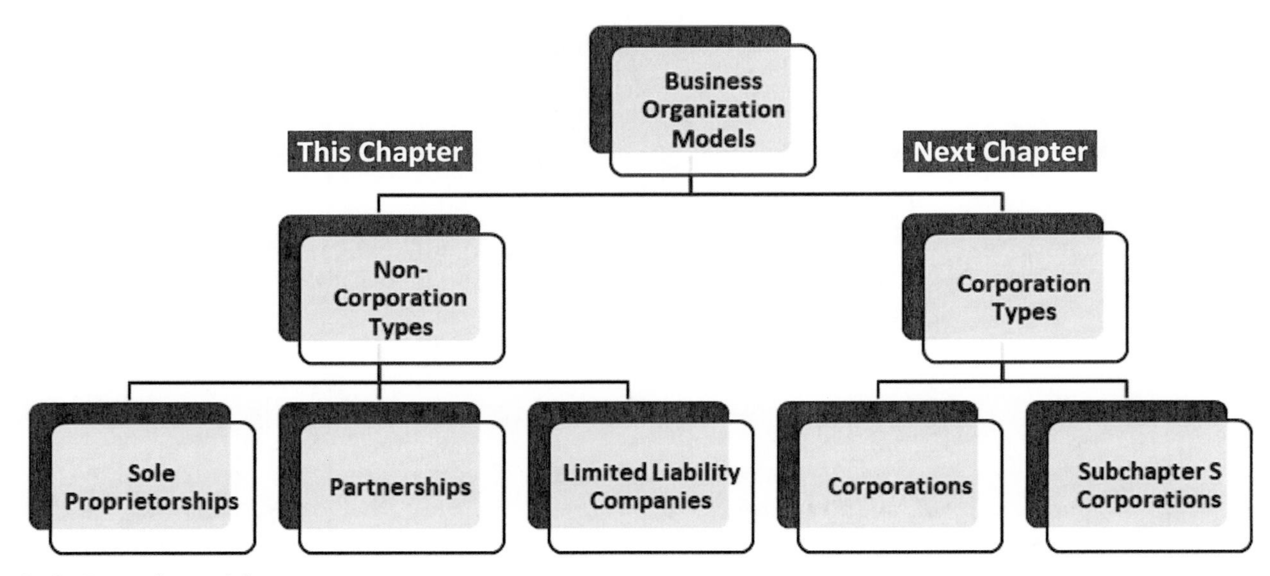

<u>Sole Proprietorships</u>
The most distinguishing feature of a **sole proprietorship** is that one person owns all the assets of the business; however, this also means that same person then has an unlimited personal **liability** for all of the activities undertaken by the business. In the case of a funeral establishment, most states require the owner of a sole proprietorship – or a manager employed by the owner – be a licensed funeral director.

Creation - Unlike many of the other business types – such as a corporation – a sole proprietorship does not need to be formally created as a separate entity apart from the owner. The owner and the business are treated as one and the same. Nonetheless, the owner may need to obtain a local business license or permit to operate in a particular municipality or state.

The business structure itself has very little government oversight; however, the activities of the business may be subject to considerable oversight. Such is the case with funeral establishments that are usually heavily regulated by the states and must follow very specific rules and regulations when offering funeral goods and services to consumers. A few of the larger municipalities in the United States also regulate certain activities of a funeral establishment, especially those regulations related to consumer protections.

Management - The owner of a sole proprietorship exercises unilateral control over the management and operation of all business activities and operations.

Ownership - The owner of a sole proprietorship may sell the operation of the business to another person or entity, in which case the sole proprietorship is terminated, and the new owner is free to create a new sole proprietorship under their own name or choose some other business type, such as a partnership.

A sole proprietorship is terminated when the owner:

- ceases or abandons all further business activities;
- files for personal bankruptcy; or
- becomes disabled, retires, or dies.

Name - If a business is going to be operating under a name different than that of the sole proprietor, the business name may have to be filed and registered with an appropriate level of government. In most cases, the name is filed as an 'assumed name' or DBA – the abbreviation for 'doing business as.'

The sole proprietor of a funeral home business with a DBA filing might list the company name on business records, checks, or signage similar to this:

Jerry J. Jones
Licensed Funeral Director
d/b/a Triple J Funeral Home
123 Main Street
Fort Riley, NK 98765

Profits and losses - The sole owner is entitled to all of the profits generated by the business, but is also personally liable for any debts incurred or losses suffered by the business.

Taxation - Because a sole proprietor business is not a separate entity from the owner, the company itself is not required to file taxes. The profit or loss from the business is reported by the owner on their personal tax return by including a *Schedule C, Profit or Loss from Business* document. This two-page form is published by the U.S. Internal Revenue Service and requires business owners to record information about their profits and losses for the tax filing year, with profits being income and losses being any expenses over $1,000 that did not incur a greater profit.

Liability - When operating any business type, consideration must be given to the liability of the owner(s) for business debts and actions. In a sole proprietorship, the liability exposure is *unlimited.* As noted earlier, the owner and the business are treated as one and the same, meaning all assets of the business and all assets of the owner are open to any claims for an injury or loss.

For example, if a family member were to get injured when a casket falls off a rack in the casket selection room, they could sue the funeral establishment and owner for damages. If they win the lawsuit and are awarded compensatory damages – and assets of the funeral establishment are not sufficient to pay the award – the court could authorize the taking of *personal* assets from the sole proprietor, such as a personally owned car or bank savings account to pay the award.

Partnerships

Creation - A **partnership** is the voluntary association of two or more people who have combined their resources – as co-owners – to carry on a lawful enterprise for their joint profit. This definition is derived from the Uniform Partnership Act (UPA) of 1997, as updated in 2013. The act is a model law written by the National Conference of Commissioners on Uniform State Laws and intended to achieve uniformity in regulating the creation and operation of business partnerships in the United States.

As of this writing, roughly 90% of the states and U.S. territories have adopted the Act since it was first released in 1914, and the majority of those states and territories have also adopted the 2013 updated version. This brings a broad uniformity and consistency to how business partnerships are created and treated all across the United States.

There are no formal steps required to create a partnership and the business is usually operated pursuant to the terms of a written partnership agreement, although the agreement does not necessarily need to be in writing. If two or more people have joint ownership of a business; share the profits and losses; and have equal rights to the management and operation of the business – they have a partnership business. Once a partnership has been created, it becomes an entity that stands alone for the purposes of such matters as property taxes and liability exposure.

In the case of a funeral establishment, many states require all – or a majority of all – partners be licensed funeral directors.

Name - There are no general requirements or prohibitions on the naming of a partnership funeral establishment business, but some states may require the names of the partners be on business records, checks, or signage similar to this:

Maple Funeral Home
Richard J. Smith
Susan L. Barber
Business Partners
Licensed Funeral Directors
123 Main Street
Fort Riley, NK 98765

Types of partners - There are two *primary* types of partners in a partnership business: general and limited. A **general partner** is an individual partner actively and openly engaged in the business and held to everyone as a partner. A **limited partner** is an individual partner whose liability for the debts of the firm is limited to the amount of his or her investment. In some states, a limited partner may also be known as a **silent partner**, defined similarly to a limited partner as an individual partner who takes no active part in the management of a partnership but has capital invested. There are subtle differences among the states between limited and silent partners.

In addition to the two primary partner types, a partnership may have one or more secret partners. A secret partner is simply a member whose name is kept secret from the public. As an example, a business partner whose name is readily recognized by the public and has a negative connotation associated with it may be a silent partner to protect the integrity and reputation of the company.

Taxation - As an entity itself, a partnership is required to file an annual tax return to report the income and expenses of the business. The *U.S. Return of Partnership Income* (Form 1065) filed with the Internal Revenue Service must include the profit (or loss) for each partner based on the terms of the partnership agreement. The partners are then required to include this information on their individual tax returns and pay any required taxes. The partnership itself does not pay any tax. This taxing mechanism is called a tax pass-through. The partnership passes the income through to the partners for income tax purposes.

Operations - A partnership agreement enumerates the duties, rights, and liabilities of the partners. Many of these requirements are developed around provisions in the UPA. For example, Section 401(a) of the UPA states, "*Each partner has equal rights in the management and conduct of the partnership's business*."

Duties of partners - A partnership agreement may include any or all of these common partner duties and responsibilities:

- be loyal and act in good faith on behalf of the partnership and not engage in other work or activities that would infringe on the partner's time and availability;
- maintain the confidentiality of business operations, records, and trade secrets;
- exercise reasonable care, skill, and due diligence in all partnership matters;
- maintain compliance with the partnership agreement or contract;
- keep other members informed of matters affecting the partnership;
- actively participate in the management of the business; and
- prepare and maintain records and documents pertaining to the operation of the partnership.

Rights of partners - A partnership agreement may include any of these partner rights:

- to be informed by other partners on all matters affecting the partnership;
- to actively participate in the management of the business;
- access to the accounting books used to record the financial transactions of the partnership;
- to share in the profits of the partnership;

- to contribution, meaning a partner that has paid more than the other partners share in a liability has a right to be repaid;

- to draw and receive advances on profits; and

- to file a suit against other partners if they break the duties and responsibilities in the partnership agreement.

Liabilities - A partner would have the authority to enter into **contracts** on behalf of the partnership when given such authority in either the partnership agreement or by consensus of the partners. As such, all partners are then liable for the contracts entered into by the authorized partner.

If it is later determined a partner did not have the authority to enter into a contract on behalf of the partnership, the other partners may then be able to limit their exposure. This would especially be true if the contract covered the purchase of goods or services unrelated to the operation of the partnership business.

Torts - A **tort** is a private or civil wrong against a person or his or her property, other than by **breach of contract**, for which there may be action for damages. As noted previously, a partnership is an entity that stands alone for the purposes of liability. Therefore, a tort claim may be filed against a partnership; a partnership and one or more of the partners; or only one or more of the partners. Depending on the state of jurisdiction, any of these actions may expose all of the partners to liability for paying any settlement or awards that result from the civil action.

Debts - All general partners are liable for the debts of the partnership; while for limited partners, liability for the debt of the business is limited to the amount of their investment.

Any new partner joining the business may only be held liable for debts incurred *after* they became members. Partners that have dissociated (removed) themselves from the partnership continue to be liable for debts incurred when they were a partner, but not for debts after they have dissociated themselves from the business.

Dissolution - The **dissolution** of a partnership is the closure of all business activities and the termination of the company. There are three methods to accomplishing a dissolution.

1. By acts of the parties.

2. By operation of law.

3. By court order.

1. Dissolution by acts of the parties - The acts of the parties may be as simple as the agreement of all the partners to dissolve the business. In other cases, the partnership may have a term of duration written in the partnership agreement calling for operations to cease and dissolution to take place on a set date.

The forced dissolution of a partnership by an act of the parties might also include the decision of a partner to voluntarily withdraw from the company; however – in those states that have adopted the UPA – the withdrawal of a partner does not usually in and of itself end the partnership. A partnership may also be dissolved when a partner is expelled from the company. Departing partners under any circumstances are liable for all existing partnership obligations prior to their leaving.

2. Dissolution by court order - There are several different factual patterns or foundations upon which a court may take notice and provide for the legal dissolution of a partnership pursuant to a court order. To accomplish this, a civil action would have to be brought before the court and the parties to the action given the opportunity to be heard. After receiving and giving consideration to the evidence presented, the court may find the proper remedy before them is the dissolution of the partnership.

A court may provide for the dissolution of a partnership on any grounds when deemed just and equitable for the parties. Common grounds for dissolution by court order may center around any of these four core issues: insanity, incapacity, misconduct, and futility

Insanity - As a mental illness or mental state, insanity is a condition of such intensity that a person cannot conduct their own affairs. In many cases, those suffering from insanity may not have the capacity to communicate rationally and sensibly with others. Individuals afflicted with this illness may be described as being of unsound mind or suffering from psychosis.

Incapacity - The issue of incapacity most often reflects on the physical condition and ability of a person to perform tasks and duties, often focused on employment obligations and responsibilities. Incapacity may be the result of an injury or illness that can be temporary or permanent and may, in some cases, be severe enough to justify the legal dissolution of a partnership by court order.

Misconduct - Misconduct of a partner may take different forms, including such activities as:

- the continuing and intentional breach of the partnership agreement, especially as that conduct may relate to managing the affairs of the company;
- engaging in conduct outside the partnership that negatively impacts or exposes the partnership to undue scrutiny or ridicule;
- engaging in criminal conduct that may call into question the reputation, standing, and integrity of the partnership and thereby has the potential to hinder and prejudice the continuing and future endeavors of the company; and
- conduct that makes it impossible for the partnership to continue if the partner remains a member of the company.

Futility - In some cases, it may be determined the continuation of a partnership is simply pointless and beyond reach. This could occur when it becomes clear the only way for a company to remain in business would be to continue operating at a loss. Another circumstance under which it might be futile to remain in business would be if it is evident that significant conflicts, disagreements, and differences exist between the partners that are irreconcilable.

3. Dissolution by operation of law - West's Encyclopedia of American Law describes 'operation of law' as:

> *Operation of Law*
>
> *The manner in which an individual acquires certain rights or liabilities through no act or cooperation of his or her own, but merely by the application of the established legal rules to the particular transaction.*
>
> *For example, when an individual dies intestate* [without a will], *the laws of descent and distribution provide for the inheritance of the estate by the heir. The property of the deceased is said to be transferred by operation of law.* *[Bracketed material by author.]*

A partnership may face dissolution as an operation of law in any of these circumstances:

- if for any reason continuing the business would be illegal;
- the bankruptcy of the partnership or, in most cases, the bankruptcy of a partner; or
- the death of a partner.

With respect to the death of a partner, in Barron's Business Law, Robert W. Emerson notes that under the revised UPA:

> *... there is no "new" partnership just because of membership changes, such as via resignation, retirement, disability or death.*
>
> *The partnership obligations of a dead partner pass to his estate. This rule follows the general requirement that dissolution not eliminate a partner's partnership liabilities. However, creditors for other debts have claims to the partner's estate before the estate pays claims from partnership creditors.*

Limited Liability Companies

As a business type, the **limited liability company** (LLC) is relatively new. The first LLC in the United States was not formed until the late 1970s in the state of Wyoming, and it was not until 1996 that the National Conference of Commissioners on Uniform State Laws issued the first rendition of the Limited Liability Company Act (LLCA). The act was revised in 2006 and is now identified as RLLCA. As of this writing, 21 states have adopted the RLLCA and two others are in the process of doing so; however, all 50 states recognize an LLC as a legal business type and have regulations in place for their creation and operation.

An LLC is a hybrid form of business that combines features of both the corporation and partnership types. It is more closely aligned with the dynamics of a partnership, but provides some of the personal liability protections previously only available to corporate structured businesses.

Creation - An application to create an LLC is accomplished by submitting what are known as Articles of Organization to the state in which the company is going to conduct business. The articles identify basic information about the LLC, such as the name under which it going to conduct business and the names of the owners – known as members. In most states, only one person (member) is needed to create an LLC. When a funeral establishment is being operated as an LLC, some states require one or all of the members be a licensed funeral director. In other states, they require each funeral home operated under the LLC umbrella to have a manager that is a licensed funeral director.

Once an LLC is created, the members most often adopt an operating agreement that serves as the by-laws or rules and regulations that provide for the more detailed operation of the company, such as enumerating the powers and duties of a manager or the procedure a member may follow to call a meeting of the full membership. Not all states require an LLC have an operating agreement.

Name - In most states, an LLC must include 'limited liability company' or 'LLC' in the name of the business, and the state where the articles of organization are filed will not allow two companies in the same state to have or use the same name.

The members of a limited liability funeral home business might list the company name on business records checks, or signage similar to this:

Brown Funeral Home, LLC
Michael Baker
Licensed Funeral Director

123 Main Street
Fort Riley, NK 98765

Management - The members of an LLC may manage the company themselves or choose to hire a manager as an employee to run the company for them.

Profits and losses - Profits and losses are shared proportionally with the members based on the distribution terms in the operating agreement, and the distributions are reported on the annual tax return of the LLC. Similar to a partnership, the LLC does not pay any taxes, as the profits and losses are passed through to the members who are then responsible for reporting the income on individual tax returns.

Taxation - For tax purposes, the federal government treats a one-member LLC as a sole proprietorship, and the owner must file taxes as described earlier in the section titled, *Sole Proprietorships*.

The IRS treats an LLC with more than one member as a partnership, and the individual members must file taxes the same as a partner would in a partnership business as described earlier in the partnership section titled, *Partnerships*. The LLC itself must file a tax return but is not subject to paying any taxes.

Liability - As the name of this business type suggests, liability is limited for the members of an LLC. Unlike a sole proprietorship or partnership, the personal assets of the members are shielded from liability claims made against the company. Any exposure a member may have is limited to the investments they have made in the company. As discussed in the next chapter, this protection is similar to the protections enjoyed by shareholders in a corporation and – for the LLC – one of the most significant advantages over other business organization types.

Chapter 16: Corporation Business Organizations

Overview

The previous chapter explored the non-corporation types of business organizations available to a funeral director seeking to open a funeral establishment. This chapter continues the review by exploring the other types of ownership and business operations that are founded on the principals of a corporation.

Chapter Definitions

Alien corporation - one that is incorporated in a foreign country.

Board of directors - a body of persons elected by the stockholders to define and establish corporate policy.

Close (closely held) corporation - a corporation in which outstanding shares of stock and managerial control are held by a limited number of people (often members of the same family).

Corporation - a business entity created by statutory law and owned by individuals known as shareholders.

Domestic corporation - operates in the state that granted the charter.

Foreign corporation - a corporation that operates in a state other than where it is chartered.

Private corporation - a corporation formed to carry out some non-governmental function.

Promoter - a person or entity that acts on behalf of a corporation to devise and implement a plan for its formation [by Author].

Public corporation - a corporation formed to carry out government functions.

Stockholders (shareholders) - those having title to one or more shares of stock in a corporation; combined, they represent ownership of the corporation.

Subchapter S corporation - business organization in which shareholders are taxed as a partnership (no double taxation) without losing corporation status.

Business Organization Models

A funeral director planning to open and operate a funeral establishment needs to consider the types of business organization models available to them in their home state. Only by the close examination of the pros and cons for each will they be in a position to determine the type most advantageous to their goals and objectives for the business they envision. The chart that follows illustrates the types of business organization models that were reviewed in the previous chapter and those that are to be reviewed in this chapter.

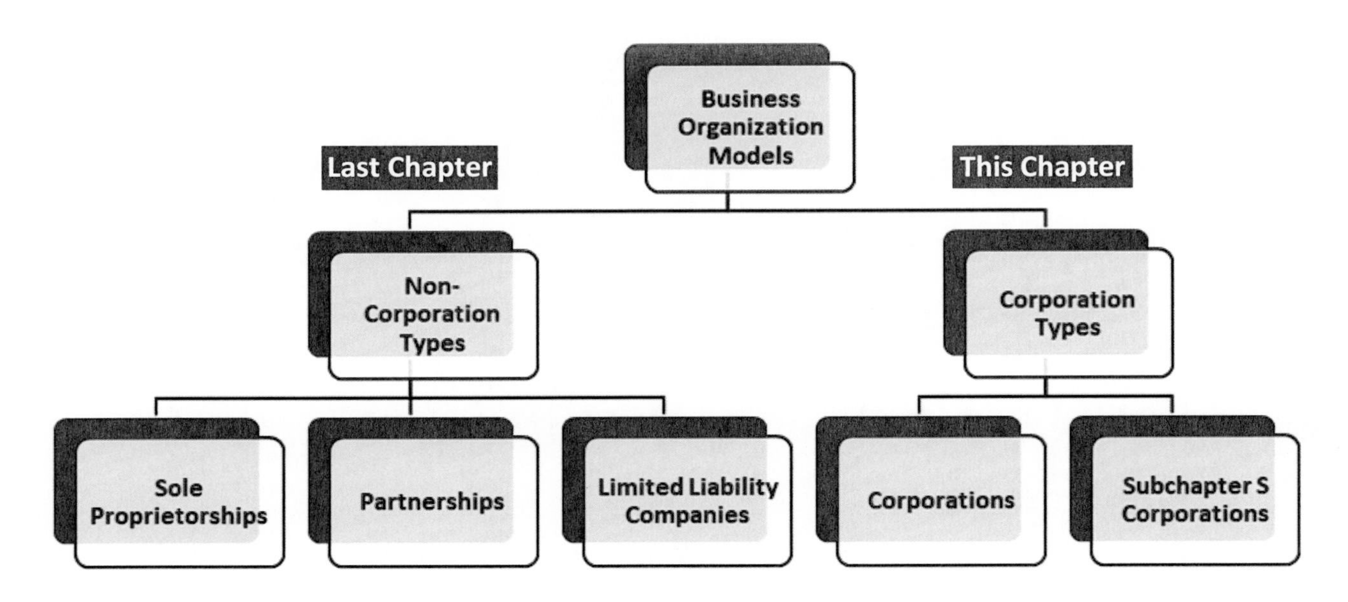

Corporations

A **corporation** is a business entity created by statutory law and owned by individuals known as shareholders. The Internal Revenue Service describes a corporation as, "*a legal entity that is separate and distinct from its owners*."

In Barron's Business Law, Robert W. Emerson explains the significance of a corporation being a separate legal entity:

> *A corporation is an artificial being created by operation of law. This artificial being, or entity, is entirely separate from its shareholders, directors, officers, and employees. This separation gives the corporation a life of its own and the responsibility and accountability to the law that are attributable to a natural person.*

A corporation may be treated as a person for almost all of the same legal purposes as an actual person or human being. It may engage in such activities as:

- owning property;
- filing civil claims against other persons or entities;
- having civil claims filed against them; and
- entering into legally binding contractual relationships with others.

A corporation can even be subject to having criminal charges filed against it. Upon conviction of a criminal offense, a corporation may be subject to monetary fines and penalties, as well as limitations being imposed on the business activities it may continue to employ. In serious breaches of law – civil or criminal – a corporation may have their charter and authority to operate as a business suspended or revoked by a state government or court of law.

Limited liability - As a completely separate entity, a corporation has a life of its own. It has its own assets, files its own taxes, and in most cases will have a perpetual existence. The corporate owners – shareholders – are generally not liable for the actions of the corporation as long as the corporation is operated pursuant to its charter and the shareholders do not commit any illegal or wrongful acts on behalf of the corporation.

Taxation - A corporation is required to file tax returns and pays taxes on any profits before passing on those profits to a certain class of shareholders in the form of a dividend. Unlike a partnership or limited liability company where profits and losses are passed directly through to the owners, *both* the corporation and the stockholders (owners) pay income taxes (double taxation). As explained by the IRS:

> *A corporation conducts business, realizes net income or loss, pays taxes and distributes profits to shareholders. The profit of a corporation is taxed to the corporation when earned, and then is taxed to the shareholders when distributed as dividends. This creates a double tax.*

Note: Incorporation is the act of creating a corporation. In naming a corporation, the abbreviation for incorporated [Inc.] may be used; or the abbreviation for corporation [Corp.] may be used. There is no legal distinction or advantage to using either of these abbreviations or names.

Classifications and Types

Private vs. public - The distinction between a public or **private corporation** is centered around whether or not it is formed to carry out some government function. When it does serve a government function, it is a **public corporation**; when it does not, it is a private corporation.

For example, the Federal Deposit Insurance Corporation (FDIC) is an independent agency created by the U.S. Congress to maintain stability and public confidence in the nation's financial system. As it serves a government function, it is classified as a public corporation.

There are some entities that may encompass characteristics of both a private and public corporation and are known as quasi-public corporations. Daniel Liberto, in an article on the Investopedia website, describes them as follows:

> *A quasi-public corporation is a company in the private sector that is supported by the government with a public mandate to provide a given service. Examples include telegraph and telephone companies, oil and gas, water, and electric light companies, and irrigation companies.*
>
> *Most quasi-public corporations began as government agencies, but have since become separate entities. They are often also referred to as public service corporations.*

While the far majority of corporations are for profit – charitable and not-for-profit organizations may create corporations to be eligible for the tax benefits and concessions many states afford to these special groups.

Domestic, foreign and alien corporations - A corporation that operates in the same state where the corporation was initially formed is called a **domestic corporation**; and, when that same corporation is operating in any other state, it is called a **foreign corporation**. These distinctions are important for the purposes of establishing which state and municipal government authorities have jurisdiction over a corporation for such matters as taxes and regulatory control.

A corporation formed in a foreign country is called an **alien corporation**.

Closely held corporation - A **close, or closely held corporation** is one in which outstanding shares of stock and managerial control are held by a limited number of people (often members of the same family). For example, Great Lake Cheese Company, Inc., was founded in 1958 and today still remains privately owned – closely held – by the Epprecht Family. The business operates eight plants across five states and provides cheese products all over the United States.

The Cornell Law School Legal Information Institute defines a closed corporation and identifies the benefits of this corporation type as follows:

> *A closed corporation is a company whose shares are held by a select few individuals who are usually closely associated with the business.*
>
> *Benefits of a Close Corporation*
>
> *The main benefit of a closely held corporation is that it will be exempt from a number of the formal rules which usually govern corporations. The specifics vary by state, but usually a close corporation must not be publicly traded, and must have fewer than a set number of shareholders (usually 35 or so). A close corporation can generally be run directly by the shareholders (without a formal board of directors and without a formal annual meeting).*

Subchapter S corporation - A **subchapter S corporation** is a business organization in which shareholders are taxed as a partnership (no double taxation) without losing corporation status. In practice, these corporations pass corporate income, losses, deductions, and credits through to their shareholders for federal tax purposes. It is then the responsibility of the shareholders to whom the pass-throughs have been made to report the income and losses on their personal tax returns, for which they are assessed tax at their individual income tax rates. This mechanism allows these corporations to avoid double taxation on the corporate income.

To qualify as a subchapter S corporation, the business must meet the following requirements:

- Be a domestic corporation.
- Have only allowable shareholders, meaning they may be individuals, certain trusts, and estates but may not be partnerships, corporations or non-resident alien shareholders.
- Have no more than 100 shareholders.

- Have only one class of stock.

Some corporate businesses, such as certain financial institutions and insurance companies, may not be eligible for status as a chapter S corporation.

Formation

Regulatory compliance - Anyone contemplating the formation of a corporation needs to be familiar with regulatory compliance issues at both the federal and state government levels. Following the stock market crash in the fall of 1929, public confidence in the markets dropped dramatically. To restore this confidence and support future markets, congress passed the Securities and Exchange Act and created the U.S. Securities and Exchange Commission (SEC).

The SEC states the commission has a three-part mission:

1. Protect investors.

2. Maintain fair, orderly, and efficient markets.

3. Facilitate capital formation.

The initial formation of a corporation and the operations that follow when the corporate charter is approved are closely monitored and regulated by both the SEC and the state government in which the corporation is being formed.

Promoter - A **promoter** organizes and guides others in the initial formation of a corporation. The promoter may be a person or an organization and seeks to find interested parties for the purpose of raising capital funds and securing the investments needed to formally create the corporation. They may offer such enticements as stocks, bonds, limited partnerships, and independent investments.

When acting on behalf of the new corporation, a promoter has a fiduciary duty and obligation to act for the benefit and in the best interests of the corporation.

Julia Kagan, on the Investopedia website, defines fiduciary as:

> *... a person or organization that acts on behalf of another person or persons, putting their clients' interest ahead of their own, with a duty to preserve good faith and trust. Being a fiduciary thus requires being bound both legally and ethically to act in the other's best interests.*

Charter - An application to formally create a corporation is submitted by the founders – also known as incorporators – to the state government in which the corporate headquarters is to be located. The application will include a proposed charter, sometimes known as 'articles of organization' or simply 'corporate charter.' A charter must provide a detailed description of the major elements of a corporation as they relate to the company objectives, structure, organization, and operations.

Structure

There are three primary structures associated with a corporation:

1. Stockholders.

2. Board of directors.

3. Officers.

Stockholders - Also known as shareholders, **stockholders** are entities or individuals having title to one or more shares of stock in a corporation; combined, they represent ownership of the corporation.

Adam Hayes, in an article on the Investopedia website, defines a shareholder as:

> *A shareholder, also referred to as a stockholder, is a person, company, or institution that owns at least one share of a company's stock, which is known as equity. Because shareholders are essentially owners in a company, they reap the benefits of a business' success. These rewards come in the form of increased stock valuations, or as financial profits distributed as dividends. Conversely, when a company loses money, the share price invariably drops, which can cause shareholders to lose money, or suffer declines in their portfolios' values.*

Stockholders have certain rights when it comes to the affairs of the corporation, and many of these will be mandated by state laws that regulate these business entities. These may include state laws that give stockholders the right to:

- approve the transfer or gifting of any company assets;

- inspect corporate financial and accounting records;

- receive properly executed stock certificates as evidence of ownership;

- attend corporate meetings and vote, unless denied by express agreement; and

- receive proportionate shares of profits when distributed as dividends.

State laws usually require shareholders to meet at least once a year to conduct the affairs of the corporation. These are called *annual* general meetings. If shareholders need to meet at other times for a specific purpose or circumstance, they are called *extraordinary* general meetings.

During the annual general meeting, stockholders may engage in such activities as:

- reviewing annual reports on the performance of the company;

- approving performance goals and objectives for the coming year;
- approving strategies put forth by the board of directors to meet future goals and objectives;
- making appointments to the board of directors;
- approving compensation rates, schedules, and salaries for executive positions;
- making decisions on the future payment of stock dividends;
- approving amendments to the corporate charter; and
- considering issues concerning the merger, consolidation, or sale of assets.

Before any valid and binding actions may be undertaken by shareholders at an annual meeting, a quorum of the members must be present. A quorum is a percentage of the entire membership as defined in the corporate charter. For example, if the charter specifies the required quorum for an annual meeting is 60% of the stockholders and the company has 100 stockholders – 60 of them would need to be present for the meeting to conduct any business.

A stockholder may be present for a meeting in person or by proxy. Proxy is the authority granted by a stockholder for another person to act on their behalf at a corporate meeting. By proxy, the other person is permitted to attend the meeting to represent the stockholder and cast votes on motions before the membership.

In most cases, a shareholder unable to attend a meeting designates another stockholder that is going to attend to be their proxy. The proxy then casts two ballots when voting – one for him or herself and one for the absent shareholder. By providing the option to use a proxy, the officers and managers of the corporation ensure the owners (stockholders) are fully invested and represented at the annual meeting. This is an important consideration, as the decisions and actions taken may alter the future course of the corporation and directly impact the value of company stock.

Board of directors - The **board of directors** (Board) of a corporation is the body of persons elected by the stockholders to define and establish corporate policy. The Board has a fiduciary duty and responsibility to act in the best interests of the stockholders.

Public corporations are required by law to have a Board made up of members that come from both inside and outside the company. They generally manage and have overall responsibility for the activities and business affairs of a corporation. They do not have responsibility for the day-to-day operations of the corporation, as these duties are the responsibility of the corporate officers.

The Board may perform such duties as:

- setting corporate policy;
- hiring and firing officers and senior corporate executives;

- declaring dividend payments or similar distributions to shareholders;
- working with and supervising the officers and managers of the corporation;
- setting long-range company goals and objectives;
- recommending to shareholders any changes to corporate operations; and
- ensuring compliance with corporate by-laws as approved by shareholders.

Officers - Officers of a corporation are selected, hired, and serve at the discretion of the corporate board of directors. They provide leadership for the day-to-day operation of the company pursuant to duties and responsibilities defined in the by-laws of the corporate charter. Some states may require certain officer positions in a corporation, such as a chief financial officer (CFO).

President - A president serves as the chief executive officer (CEO). This position works very closely with the corporate board of directors and often serves as the public face and spokesperson for the company. They oversee all of the day-to-day operations of the company, including having the authority to hire employees and staff as needed to meet the demands of the company.

Vice president - A corporation will have a vice president to serve as second in command of the day-to-day operations and officially represent the president when needed. Larger corporations may have several vice president positions with specific titles and tasks, such as being VP of Marketing or VP of Distribution. A senior or executive vice president position may be appointed to assist in managing multiple subordinate vice president positions.

Secretary - A secretary is another corporate officer that works very closely with the board of directors. The position handles such duties as:

- maintaining the books, records, and files of the corporation;
- organizing and managing shareholder, board, and senior management meetings;
- ensuring compliance with state corporate laws; and
- serving as the primary contact for shareholder inquiries and assistance.

In smaller corporations with no in-house legal counsel, it is not unusual for a corporate secretary to be a business law attorney.

Treasurer - A treasurer is responsible for management of the corporate funds and often supervises an accounting office that handles corporate-wide financial matters, such as accounts receivable and payable and tax compliance. They may be designated as the chief financial officer of a corporation.

Classes and Types of Stock

Capital stock represents the total number of stock shares a company is authorized by the corporate charter to issue. It includes shares already sold to the public and shares held in the company treasury, known as treasury stock. Treasury stock may include shares that have not been sold or were bought back by the company.

There are typically two classes of capital stock: common and preferred. Common stock has no preference over other classes of stock, but those who own common stock have ownership in the corporation and a right to share in the profits of the business. They have shareholder rights and shareholder duties as described previously under the *Structure* section of this chapter.

Preferred stock affords the shareholder additional rights and options that may not always be available to shareholders that have common stock. Rights and options are determined by each corporation and memorialized in the charter by-laws. Typical preferences may include such rights and options as:

- priority access to the assets of the corporation if it were to be liquidated or dissolved;
- guaranteed representation on the board of directors;
- promised and/or fixed cash dividend payments;
- special or additional voting rights;
- redemption rights, meaning the right to mandate the corporation buy back the shares; and
- the right to convert their preferred stock over to common stock

Another expression related to stocks is 'par value.' This term represents the face value of a share but has no relevance to the actual market value of a share at any given time. Historically, when stocks were printed on paper, the par value was printed on the face of the certificates. Today, most corporations set the par value of a share to be one-cent to avoid any legal liability if the stock drops below its par value.

A typical stock certificate.

Dissolution

While most corporations are created and designed to have a perpetual existence, they may under normal circumstances be legally terminated by dissolution. In most states, shareholders may voluntarily dissolve a corporation by the majority approval of a resolution authorizing the dissolution and then filing it with the Secretary of State in the state that issued the company's certificate of incorporation.

Shareholders may also petition a court to dissolve the corporation in special circumstances. For example, the board of directors may be operating the business illegally or unlawfully, or the shareholders may be deadlocked on an issuing requiring shareholder approval, including dissolution.

Creditors may also ask a court to intervene when the company cannot pay its debts and the unpaid creditors have been awarded a court judgment for money owed to them by the corporation. By dissolving the company, the creditors can then petition the court to seize the assets of the corporation for the purposes of paying any outstanding debt claims and satisfying any outstanding court awarded judgments.

Chapter 17: Real Property Law

<u>Overview</u>
Property laws define and govern rights and protections related to the ownership of property. They provide for the right of the owner to use, profit from, sell, transfer, protect, alter, abandon, or even destroy the property. This chapter identifies the acceptable and legally protected means to own *real* property, and the remedies available to address any failure to adhere to legal requirements associated with ownership.

<u>Chapter Definitions</u>
Debtor - a person or entity that owes money to another.

Deed - document conveying title to real property.

Fee simple estate - the broadest form of ownership in real property.

Life estate - interest in real property for duration of a person's life.

Mortgage - a secured loan on a parcel of real property.

Negligence - failure to exercise reasonable care.

Personal property - all property which is not real property.

Real property - land and those objects permanently attached to land.

Secured claim - a debt which is supported by a pledge, mortgage or lien on assets belonging to the debtor.

<u>Property - Generally</u>
There are two types of property: real and personal. **Real property** is land and those objects permanently attached to land; and **personal property** is all property which is not real property.

Jean Folger, in an article on the Investopedia website, describes real property as:

> *Real property is the land, everything that is permanently attached to the land, and all of the rights of ownership, including the right to possess, sell, lease, and enjoy the land. Real property can be classified according to its general use as residential, commercial, agricultural, industrial, or special purpose. In order to understand if you have the right to sell your home, you need to know which rights you possess – or don't possess – in the property.*

<u>Estates in Real Property</u>
The terms real property and real estate are for all practical purposes interchangeable, but when speaking about real property, the phrase '*estates in real property*' specifically refers to the type, kind, or extent of the ownership a person has in real property.

The two most common types of estates in real property are:

1. Freehold, those in which there is *ownership* of real property; and

2. Non-freehold, those that involve the *leasing*, but not ownership of real property.

Freehold Estates

Freehold estates may last forever – known as a fee simple estate; or last for a lifetime – known as a life estate.

Fee simple estate - The **fee simple estate** is the broadest form of ownership in real property and provides the most widespread interest in real property. Fee simple means unconditional ownership. The owner may do anything they want with the property, such as build structures on it, sell it, or provide for its transfer to another upon their death. These estates are considered perpetual and ownership automatically passes to the legal heirs of the owner when the owner dies if no other provisions have been made

Life estate - A **life estate** grants interest and ownership in real property limited to a term or duration of life.

For example, a son may grant a life estate for his mother to own and possess real property, but her ownership of the property is limited to the duration of her lifetime. She would not be permitted to sell the property and also would assume responsibility for maintaining it.

In most states, the deed transferring property provides for the occupant to possess and use the property for the duration of their lifetime, after which ownership passes back to the original owner or some other named person to whom a life estate would be granted. In the previous example, following the death of the mother, the deed and right to possession and ownership would pass back to her son or could pass to some other person(s), such as her grandchildren. Life estates may be referred to as a 'tenant for life' or 'life tenant' ownership.

Joint ownership - There are three possible forms of tenancy with respect to the *ownership* and possession of real property by two or more individuals, including:

1. Joint tenancy - When a joint tenancy is created all of the tenants (owners) have equal rights and obligations with respect to the real property. Most importantly, if any of the joint tenancy owners dies, their share of the ownership is distributed among the surviving tenants. This concept is known as a 'right of survivorship.' To legally create a joint tenancy in property relationship, the prospective owners must meet what are known in the legal community as the four unities:

   (1) Unity of time - The property interest must be attained by all of the tenants at the same time.

   (2) Unity of title - The property interests for all tenants must all be contained in the same instrument, such as a deed or title.

(3) Unity of interest - All tenants must have the same interest type. Interests are rights, claims, or privileges an individual has toward real estate.

(4) Unity of possession - All tenants must have the right to possess the whole property.

2. Tenancy in common - This form of ownership is most frequently used when the real property owners are not married to each other. In this joint relationship, each party exclusively owns their own share of the property. Shares may or may not be proportionally equal, as the terms of the ownership are most often agreed upon by the owners and memorialized in the deed or other legal document. If no record of share distribution is described or known, it is usually presumed the shares are equal for each party. With a tenancy in common, any tenant may sell their share of the ownership without the need for the other tenant(s) to sell their shares at the same time.

3. Tenancy by the entirety - As of this writing, this joint ownership of real property option is only available to married couples, and less than half of the states recognize this type of ownership. It is similar to a joint tenancy in that the requirements of the four unities must be met, and it provides the same right of survivorship. In most cases, this type of tenancy ownership may only be broken by death, a divorce, or mutual agreement of the parties to the marriage.

   Unlike a tenancy in common – where any one owner may unilaterally sell their share of the ownership – one owner in a tenancy by the entirety cannot transfer or convey their share of the real property to another. For example, if a married couple has tenancy by the entirety ownership, neither spouse may sell or transfer their share of the ownership without the other spouse also selling their share.

The four unities apply to *ownership* types of tenancy as shown here;

Unities	Joint Tenancy	Tenancy in Common	Tenancy in the Entirety
Time	X		X
Title	X		X
Interest	X		X
Possession	X	X	X

If no form of tenancy has been provided in a property deed, the law will in most cases provide for the ownership to be a tenancy in common.

Deeds and title abstracts - A **deed** is a legal document that provides for and memorializes the conveyance or transfer of property or rights from one person to another. In the case of real estate, a deed document is the mechanism used to convey and record the transfer of title – and thereby ownership – of real property from one person or entity to another person or entity.

For example: John deeded his home to his son – meaning John legally transferred the title, ownership and possession of his home to his son by deed. When a deed is signed (executed), it officially passes legal title to real property from the seller to the buyer.

A title abstract is a legal document that provides a summary of deeds and other documents that establish the ownership *history* of real property. The abstract also identifies any liens, mortgages, or other legal impediments filed or recorded against the property that might prohibit or influence the legal transfer of title and ownership from the current owner to a new owner.

Mortgages - A **mortgage** is a secured loan on a parcel of real property. It comes in the form of a legal instrument that documents the relationship between a buyer and a financial institution that lends money to the buyer. The mortgage grants the lender an interest in real estate to secure the loan. This interest is known as a **secured claim**, a debt which is supported by a pledge, mortgage, or lien on assets belonging to the **debtor** (person that owes money). The mortgage is 'secured' because the financial institution has a legal right to take possession and ownership of the property in a foreclosure proceeding if the mortgagor fails to keep up the mortgage payments.

Alert funeral service professionals will note the root word of mortgage is 'mort.' Mortgage is in fact a French legal term meaning 'death contract.' The mortgage ends (dies) when the obligation to repay the loan has been fulfilled or the real property has been foreclosed on and seized by the lender for failure to repay the debt.

Non-freehold Estates

Non-freehold estates involve the *leasing* of property. They are not inheritable and exist without any actual ownership of the real property. They may be known in some states as a leasehold estate.

Lease - A lease is the temporary transfer of the right to the possession – but not ownership – of such items as property, goods, and services. The two most common leases are for the lease of a motor vehicle, such as a rental car; and the lease of real property, such as an apartment. Leases for the right to possession of real property create a contractual relationship between the person that owns the property – called the landlord; and the person seeking to lease the property – called the tenant. A lease may be a written or oral agreement, but in both cases create a contract between the parties binding them to certain duties and obligations. Most lease types have a stated term of duration.

West's Encyclopedia of American Law describes a lease as:

> *A contractual agreement by which one party conveys an estate in property to another party, for a limited period, subject to various conditions, in exchange for something of value, but still retains ownership.*

Types of tenancy - There are four types of tenancy that may exist by agreement between a landlord and a tenant for the *lease* of real property:

1. Tenancy for years - Contrary to the name of this type of tenancy, the duration of the lease does not have to be in years. It can be for any number of days, weeks, or years, or any other stated period of time. It must however have a definite and fixed duration stated in the lease, after which the agreement automatically terminates. If the term of the lease agreement is one year or more, it must be in writing based on the Statute of Frauds. This statute is a legal concept requiring certain contractual relationships be in writing, including contracts for:

   - the sale of real property;
   - the purchase of goods worth over $500; and
   - those lasting one year or more, which may include a lease contract for real property.

2. Periodic tenancy - Also known as a period-to-period tenancy, the periodic tenancy has an indefinite duration, as the term of the lease renews automatically if neither party notifies the other of the intent to terminate the tenancy. The wording used in the agreement to identify the term of the lease will be non-specific in nature, such as stating the term runs 'from month to month' instead of specifying exact dates, such as monthly from January 1, 2021 to December 31, 2021.

   This is one of the most common tenancy types for leasing business space for commercial purposes; or the rental of an apartment or house for residential purposes. To terminate a periodic tenancy, the landlord or the tenant must give advance notice to the other. If the term is week to week, they must give one week notice; month to month, one month's notice; or year to year, a six-month notice.

3. Tenancy at will - Also known as an estate at will, a tenancy at will has no fixed time period, term, or stated duration. The tenancy remains in place as long both the landlord and tenant agree. The agreement may be terminated at any time – *at will* – by either party by giving notice to the other. Some states specify the length of advance notice required to terminate the agreement, while others mandate 'reasonable' notice be given.

4. Tenancy at sufferance - This special tenancy is created when a tenant remains in possession of real property beyond the duration specified in the lease agreement without any legal right to do so or consent of the landlord. Having initially entered and taken possession of property *legally and lawfully* differentiates the tenant from a common trespasser. A trespasser enters *illegally and remains unlawfully* on property.

   By declaring a tenancy at sufferance relationship, the law permits the landlord to continue – or at least attempt to continue – collecting rent. This type of tenancy may be terminated by the landlord following the legal process for an eviction to have the tenant removed; or by establishing a new tenancy relationship with the tenant.

In summary, the four types of tenancy for the *lease* of real property are:

Tenancy for Years
• Right to occupy real property for a definite or fixed period of time.
Periodic Tenancy
• A tenancy that continues for successive fixed periods.
Tenancy at Will
• Interest in real property that continues indefinitely.
Tenancy at Sufferance
• When a tenant does not leave the premises after the tenancy expires.

Landlord and Tenant Duties and Responsibilities

All states have laws, rules, and regulations listing the duties and responsibilities of the parties to a landlord-tenant lease agreement. While they vary to some degree in their particulars, most address basic requirements. Landlord duties most often include:

1. Delivering the premises to the tenant in a condition of habitability. The property must have such functional services and characteristics as proper plumbing, running water, heat, utility services, structural integrity, waste disposal facilities, and other features needed to provide for basic human habitability.

2. Providing for the quiet enjoyment and use of the premises. This includes such activities as providing notice and receiving permission to enter the premises as needed for maintenance and repairs, and the right for the tenant to enjoy the reasonable use of the premises without any landlord interference.

3. Maintaining the functional services and characteristics as provided above in a continual state of good repair.

Tenant duties include not committing waste. In property law, waste is the unreasonable or improper use of real property by a person who has legal possession of the property. A tenant may not commit any of these three wastes:

1. Voluntary waste - This waste occurs when the tenant *intentionally acts* with the result being damage to the property, such as intentionally breaking a window or damaging woodwork. This waste also includes the removal of any real property fixtures or attachments, such as a tenant removing a bathtub that was attached to the floor and taking it with them when they vacate the property. Voluntary waste may also be known in some states as affirmative waste.

2. Permissive waste - While voluntary waste occurs when someone *acts*, permissive waste exists when a tenant *fails to act* to prevent damage or harm to the real property, either physically or financially. The failure to exercise reasonable care is a form of **negligence** that causes waste.

   For example, a tenant would be negligent if damage or harm (waste) were to occur due to failure to maintain the property in the same condition as when first taking possession. Another example would be the failure of the tenant to report a broken water pipe that then floods the basement and damages a furnace.

3. Ameliorating waste - This waste occurs when a tenant makes unauthorized improvements, renovations, or alterations to the real property, even if those changes increase the value of the property. A tenant has possession rights to real property but not ownership rights. As such, they cannot make changes to the land, structures, or other objects making up the real property without the permission of the owner or future interest holders.

   Ameliorating waste would occur if a tenant were to build an in-ground swimming pool on the property, cut down trees on the land, or affix a ceiling fan fixture in a bedroom. These actions would interfere with the superior right of the owner to make decisions on improvements to the real property for themselves. For example, the property owner may have had plans to build a storage building on the same location where the tenant built the swimming pool.

Note: See the chapter titled, *Personal Property*, for information on when a personal property object – such as a ceiling fan – becomes a real property object.

A tenant also has a duty to pay rent in a timely manner. A lease agreement typically enumerates the obligations of both the landlord and the tenant, including the duty and responsibility of the tenant to pay rent by a certain date on a scheduled basis.

Chapter 18: Personal Property Law

Overview

The previous chapter explored property law as it relates to the ownership and possession of real property. This chapter continues the discussion on property law by exploring the dynamics and elements that make up the body of laws related to personal property.

Chapter Definitions

Bailee - the party who acquires possession, but not the title, of another's personal property, under agreement.

Bailment - the transfer of possession, but not the title of another's personal property, under agreement.

Bailor - the party who gives up possession, but not the title, of personal property in a bailment.

Common carrier - any carrier required by law to convey passengers or freight without refusal if the approved fare or charge is paid (airline, train, etc.)

Deed - document conveying title to real property.

Fixture - objects permanently attached to land.

Gross negligent act - the intentional failure or the reckless disregard of the consequences with respect to conduct affecting the life or property of another.

Liability - responsibility for actions and/or other debts; the quality or state of being legally obligated or accountable.

Personal property - all property which is not real property.

Real property - land and those objects permanently attached to land.

Statement of Funeral Goods and Services Selected - an itemized list of goods and services that a consumer has selected during an arrangement conference that allows them to evaluate the selections and make any desired changes.

Title - ownership; evidence of ownership of property.

Property - Geneally

There are two types of property: real and personal. **Real property** is land and those objects permanently attached to land; and **personal property** is all property which is not real property.

Julia Kagan, in an article on the Investopedia website, describes personal property as:

Personal property is a class of property that can include any asset other than real estate. The distinguishing factor between personal property and real estate, or real property, is that personal property is movable; that is, it isn't fixed permanently to one particular location. It is generally not taxed like fixed property.

Personal Property

Personal property may be tangible or intangible. A person can physically hold and possess tangible property, and in most cases tangible property can be moved. This is in contrast to real property which is fixed and unmovable.

As an example, this book is tangible personal property. It can be physically held and possessed by a student or instructor. On the other hand, the contents, thoughts, ideas, descriptions, and information provided in this book are the intangible personal property of the author. Authors have what are known as intellectual property rights in the content of their books. These rights may be expressed by copyrights, patents, and trademarks.

Intangible personal property is an item of individual value that cannot be touched or held. It includes any item of worth that is not physical in nature but instead represents something else of value. In addition to intellectual property, as described above, intangible property rights exist in such items as stocks, bonds, software programs, telephone services, and utility services like gas and electricity. For example, a person who owns stock will have documentation which is evidence of their ownership, but the stock itself is intangible personal property.

Sources and Ways to Acquire Title

Title, as a term used in property law, refers to the right or evidence of a person to have ownership in either real property or personal property. For example, a person may have title to and therefore right to possession and ownership of real property by means of a **deed** that transfers title from one person to another.

Similarly, a motor vehicle is personal property, and a title document is the common method used as evidence of ownership and the right to possession of the vehicle. While these are two bright-line examples, there are several sources or ways to obtain title to personal property that may not be evidenced by a specific document or formalized transaction.

Purchase - The most common method of taking possession and title of personal property is by simply purchasing the property. An offer of money or some other form of compensation in exchange for the possession and ownership of personal property takes place thousands of times a day in retail sales. For example, purchasing food and sundry goods in a grocery store is a means to acquire legal title to the food and goods.

Purchase agreements - Purchase agreements, contracts, or other similar written documents that provide for the transfer of personal property are another way to acquire title. For example, the FTC required **Statement of Funeral Goods and Services Selected** is the means to acquire title to personal property, such as a casket or a flag display case. Purchase agreements often specify the terms and conditions of a sale and – when those have been met – the transfer of the right to possess and own personal property is complete.

Production - If someone were to produce personal property for themselves, they will have acquired ownership. For example, if someone bought wood and used it to construct bird houses to sell on Amazon, they would own and acquire title to the wood (by purchase), and then acquire ownership and title of the bird houses (by production) when they use the wood to build them.

Gift - Personal property may be gifted to someone. A gift in this sense is the voluntary transfer of personal property by one person (the donor) to another (the donee) with no compensation, consideration, or other exchange of value from the person receiving to the person giving the gift. A gift may be conditioned on some future event, such as the death of the person making the gift or the donee reaching a certain age.

The three elements to establish a legal gift are:

- the donor had the required intent;
- the property was delivered to the donee; and
- the donor excepted the gift.

Abandoned property - Property laws provide the conditions upon which the finder of abandoned property may lawfully acquire title. For the transfer or title to be legal, the previous owner must have fully intended to surrender and relinquish any legal title they had to ownership and the right to possess the property. For example, if the owner of an old lawnmower places it out in front of his home with a 'free' sign on it, the owner has abandoned the mower. If a neighbor picks it up the next day, the neighbor would immediately acquire legal title to its ownership and use.

Mislaid/lost property - Mislaid or lost property is not abandoned for the purposes of another person seeking to acquire title to the property in question. Personal property is considered to be *mislaid* if the owner *intentionally* let the property out of their possession with the intent to recover it but later forgets to retrieve it or forgets where it was placed. Personal property is considered to be *lost* if the owner has involuntarily and *unknowingly* let the property out of their possession and does not know where it is located. Both lost and mislaid property continue to be owned by the person that lost or mislaid it.

The distinction in these two terms – lost and mislaid – was historically used to require the finder of *mislaid* property to turn it into authorities; and, in the case of the finder of *lost* property, to grant them title to the property against all others except the true owner. Property laws today take a much broader viewpoint on found property, with most states now requiring found property be turned into public authorities, regardless as to whether or not it is believed to have been lost or mislaid.

Mislaid/lost property laws provide for the disposition of property that has been turned in to authorities should the owner not be located. In most cases, a state statute will grant the finder legal title to the property after a set period of time based on the value of the found property. True owners will in almost all cases have a superior right to lost or mislaid property up until a state law provides for the legal transfer of title pursuant to lost and found property statutes.

Fixtures

Personal property can in some circumstances become attached to real property, after which it is no longer considered personal property but instead a part of the real property. For example, if someone purchases a new furnace, they have acquired ownership and title to personal property – the furnace. However, if they have the furnace installed in their home by connecting it to all of the necessary utilities, duct work, and air handlers, it has become a **fixture** and thereby permanent part of the real property. A fixture in property law is defined as an object permanently attached to land.

In Barron's Business Law, Robert W. Emerson states:

> *Once personal property has become so incorporated into real property that it is difficult, costly, and/or impossible to remove, the personal property is considered a fixture.*

Bailments

A **bailment** is the delivery and transfer of the possession – but not the ownership – of personal property to another person by agreement. This person then holds the property for a certain purpose under an express or implied-in-fact contract. The person who delivers and gives up possession but not title of the personal property is the **bailor**; the person who receives possession and control over the personal property – but not ownership – is the **bailee**.

West's Encyclopedia of American Law provides the following description of a bailment:

> *The term bailment is derived from the French bailor, 'to deliver.' It is generally considered to be a contractual relationship since the bailor and bailee, either expressly or impliedly, bind themselves to act according to particular terms. The bailee receives only control or possession of the property while the bailor retains the ownership interests in it.*
>
> *During the specific period a bailment exists, the bailee's interest in the property is superior to that of all others, including the bailor, unless the bailee violates some term of the agreement. Once the purpose for which the property has been delivered has been accomplished, the property will be returned to the bailor or otherwise disposed of pursuant to the bailor's directions.*

As an example, if a family member delivers a diamond necklace to a funeral director with the expectation that it will be displayed and worn by the decedent during calling hours and then returned before burial, a bailment has been created between the parties. The family member is the bailor, as they delivered possession of the necklace to the funeral director. The funeral director is the bailee, as they have received possession and control of the necklace for a certain purpose.

Conditions - To legally establish a bailment relationship requires the following four elements and requirements:

1. Delivery - The bailor must deliver the property into the possession and control of the bailee so they may carry out the tasks, duties, or activities for which the transfer of possession is being made. Actual physical delivery is not always necessary.

   For example, if a vehicle owner parks his car at an auto repair shop and hands the keys to the owner so the car can be serviced, delivery has been accomplished. In property law, this possession is known as constructive possession or constructive custody, as compared to actual physical custody.

   In the necklace example, the family member (bailor) *delivered* the necklace to the funeral director (bailee).

2. Acceptance - The bailee must knowingly accept delivery of possession and control over the property of the bailment.

   In the necklace example, the bailee willingly and knowingly *accepted* possession and control over the necklace.

3. Purpose - The possession granted to the bailee must be for some specific purpose.

   In the necklace example, the specific purpose was for the funeral director to display the property on the decedent during calling hours.

4. Temporary - In a bailment situation, the possession and control must be temporary, with the property ultimately being returned to the bailor.

   In the necklace example, the property is to be returned to the bailor prior to the burial of the decedent.

Duty of care - Bailments may be identified as being those that:

- solely benefit the bailor;
- solely benefit the bailee; or
- are beneficial to both the bailor and the bailee.

These three benefit distinctions influence the expected duty of care for the parties. There are three levels of care commonly used in the legal community.

1. Benefit of the bailor only - Bailments that solely benefit the bailor are often called gratuitous bailments, as the bailee receiving the personal property is in many cases doing something as a favor to the bailor. The bailee receives no compensation, payment, or other thing of value, and their duty or level of care against loss or damage to the property would therefore be *minimal or slight*.

For example, Mike asks his neighbor Sam if he would allow him to store his motorcycle in Sam's shed for the winter for free. If Sam agrees, he would have a very low duty of care because there is no benefit to him. The beneficiary of this bailment is solely Mike.

Note: In a 'benefit of the bailor only' bailment, the bailee could be subject to a higher level of **liability** if they were to commit a **gross negligent act**.

2. Benefit of the bailee only - Bailments that solely benefit the bailee hold the bailee to a *high or extraordinary* duty of care to prevent damage or loss of the personal property. For example, if Joe borrows his neighbor Bills' snowblower and Bill receives no compensation, payment, or other thing of value in exchange, Joe has a high or extraordinary duty of care against any loss or damage to the snowblower.

3. Beneficial to both parties - Bailments that are beneficial to both parties are those where the bailee receives some form of compensation from the bailor in exchange for the bailee performing some service or other thing of value for the bailor. In these cases, the bailee will be held to an *ordinary and reasonable* duty of care.

   In the necklace example, the funeral director (bailee) is receiving monetary compensation (a benefit) for providing funeral services, including calling hours; and, in giving the funeral director possession and control over the necklace, the family member (bailor) has benefited by having the necklace on the decedent for the calling hours.

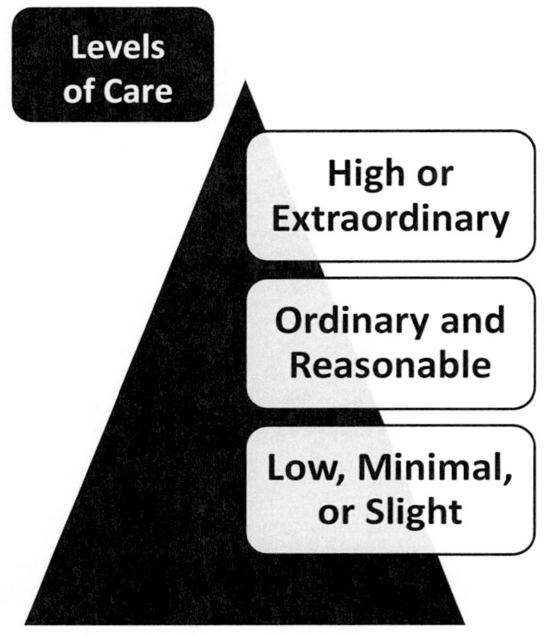

Special bailments - There are special bailments that require the bailee to exercise an extraordinary or high degree of care. Notable among them are bailment relationships that exist when consumers do business by agreement with **common carriers** or innkeepers.

Common carriers are public transportation companies required by law to convey passengers or freight without refusal if the approved fare or charge is paid. They include such organizations as airlines, railroads, trucking companies, and cargo ships. The very nature of common carriers on a daily basis is serving as bailees to take possession and exercise control over the personal property of bailors for the purposes of transportation and delivery to others.

Innkeepers are generally defined as organizations that rent rooms to the public on a temporary basis. They may be known in various state property laws as innkeepers, hotelkeepers, or hoteliers for the purposes of regulating bailments. Innkeepers may be subject to bailment requirements when they take possession and control of the personal property of their guests, such as a guests' valuables or luggage.

Many state laws impose extraordinary standards of care on common carriers and innkeepers when they have bailments with their customers. These laws impose strict liability – sometimes known as absolute liability – that allows these entities to be held liable for any loss or damage to personal property without the need to prove the act that caused the loss or damage was either intentional or negligent. With limited exceptions, these groups will be held absolutely liable.

Exceptions that would relieve a common carrier or innkeeper from being held to strict liability for loss or damage include:

1. The actions of the owner of the property (bailor), such as not properly packaging the goods for transportation by the common carrier.

2. The acts of government authorities when they cause the loss or damage, such as the government seizure of the property for criminal prosecutions.

3. An act of God, such as a hurricane or other natural disaster.

4. The acts of a public enemy, a designation that includes countries, groups, or individuals that are attempting the violent overthrow of the government.

5. The nature of the goods, to the degree the shipper should have known the risk and taken extra precautions to prevent the loss, such as the potential for the loss of perishable goods if not properly refrigerated or packaged.

The liability of a common carrier starts when personal property is delivered to them and ends when the person to whom the property is being sent takes possession. Liability would also end when the goods are removed from the carrier and stored in a warehouse or storage facility.

A common carrier can refuse to transport goods if they are unsafe or the carrier is not properly equipped to handle them, such as the transportation vehicle or other conveyance not being refrigerated or having the capacity to carry the weight of the goods.

Chapter 19: Insurance

Overview
In all business environments, it is important for owners and operators to review business operations and procedures to identify risks and exposures in the workplace. Thereafter, measures may be taken to minimize and manage those known risks. This process is known as risk management, and one measure that can be taken is to ensure there is adequate insurance coverage to cover any unexpected loss. This chapter explores the various types of insurance needs common to the funeral service industry.

Chapter Definitions
Bailee - the party who acquires possession, but not the title, of another's personal property, under agreement.

Beneficiary - recipient of the proceeds of a life insurance policy.

Indemnification - a legal agreement by one party to hold another party not liable for potential losses or damages.

Malpractice - failure to perform a professional service with the ability and care generally exercised by others in the profession.

Mortgage - a secured loan on a parcel of real property.

Term life policy - contract whereby insurer assumes the risk of death of insured for a specific time with no cash surrender.

Universal life policy - an insurance product is combining features of both whole life and term life policies.

Whole life policy - insurance that covers an insured for life and accumulates cash surrender value.

Insurance as a System
Insurance is a system to share the risk of loss among a group of people. A risk is a prediction concerning potential loss based on knowledge or unknown facts. An insurance policy is a contract where a party (the insured) shifts the risk of financial loss to a risk bearer (the insurance company) for a fee.

The policy itself is the written contract of insurance between the customer (insured) and the insurance company (insurer). There are different types of insurance policies and different premiums for the types of coverage available.

Before an insurance policy is issued, the party seeking to purchase the insurance coverage can deal with an insurance agent who works directly for an insurance company or an insurance broker who works independently and offers insurance to a customer from any one of the numerous insurance companies operating in a particular state.

Insurable Interest

A basic tenet regarding insurance is that the insured must have a financial interest in the life or property being insured. Accordingly, to purchase insurance the insured must be in a position where they could sustain a financial loss or a personal loss. Since the insurance contract agrees to assume a specific risk, if the insured has no interests to protect, there can be no acceptance of risk and therefore no insurance. Without an insurable interest, someone buying insurance is gambling a loss will occur.

Life insurance - With life insurance, an insured has an insurable interest in his or her own life; however, when someone insures the life of another, there must be a reasonable expectation of benefit for the continued well-being of the individual to have an insurable interest in that other person's life. The insurable interest must exist at the time the policy is purchased, but does not usually need to exist at the time of death of the insured. However, as Ashcroft states, if a court becomes involved and determines that, "*... an insurable interest no longer exists and the interest of the beneficiary is adverse to that of the insured, the policy could be invalidated.*"

Image courtesy of Investmentzen.[2]

Examples of relationships that can give rise to an insurable interest include those between:

- parents and children;
- husband and wife; and
- a partner and co-partner in a business.

Property insurance - To collect on a property insurance policy, an insurable interest must exist when the policy is purchased, as well as at the time of the loss.

A relationship giving rise to an insurable interest in property could be the ownership of specific personal property or real property. An insurable interest occurs when property is destroyed and the insured suffers a financial loss. Ashcroft provides these three examples of insurable interests – other than one of ownership:

> – For real property,
> *... a mortgagee would have an insurable interest in the property mortgaged to the extent of the **mortgage**.*
>
> – For personal property,
> *... a **bailee** would have an insurable interest in the property bailed up to the time of the possible loss.*

- In a partnership,
... a partner has an insurable interest in the property owned by the firm to the extent of the potential loss.

Note: See chapters titled, *Real Property Law* and *Personal Property Law*, for additional information on mortgages and bailees, respectively.

Insurance Contract
Laws governing - An insurance policy follows the general rules of a contract reviewed in previous chapters. Individual states regulate insurance contracts, and it is therefore essential funeral service practitioners familiarize themselves with insurance laws and requirements in the states where they practice. Some states may require specific clauses in an insurance policy.

Application - The party seeking to purchase an insurance policy must complete an application, and a copy is usually attached to the insurance policy. By doing so, the person applying for insurance is bound by the information they recorded on the application. The insurance company investigates to evaluate the information provided to them and determines whether or not to issue a policy. Misstatements or misrepresentations can void a policy if the insurance company can demonstrate they would not have issued the policy had they known all the facts.

Effective date - This is an important part of a policy because the effective date is the date insurance coverage begins, and the insurance company will only be able to process a claim after a formal written policy has been issued. Nevertheless, there are times when an applicant is protected between the time the application is received and the formal decision of the company. This occurs when an insurance agent issues a binder – a written temporary insurance policy. When applying for life insurance, there is usually some form of premium paid before coverage begins.

When an insurance company issues a new policy, the insured must pay the premium (a charge or fee) for the coverage. Premiums can vary depending on the coverage in the policy, and one method for keeping premium payments lower is for an insured to have a deductible. With a deductible, the insured agrees to pay a certain percentage or amount toward any loss incurred. The higher deductible an insured agrees to pay, the lower the premium charge.

Indemnification - When a claim is filed for any loss or damage, the insurance company is required to provide **indemnification** for its insured, meaning the insurer will pay any damages to the person who was damaged or injured within applicable policy limits.

Provisions and Clauses
Insurance policies are specific regarding the coverages they provide, the risks they cover, and the risks they exclude. These are made clear in a policy by the inclusion of clauses, provisions, and declarations. Some of the more common are provided here.

Face value - An insurance policy is issued for a stated dollar amount the insurance company will pay for a loss. In the case of a life insurance policy, it may be known as a death benefit. The higher the face value of an insurance policy, the higher the premium (cost).

Coinsurance clause - A coinsurance clause is standard in fire insurance, homeowner policies, and health insurance. They provisions set limits on the payment for a loss or claim.

For example, if an owner insures property for a specified percentage of its value – typically 80% – the insured may recover any loss up to the face amount of the policy. On the other hand, if the insurance coverage is less than a fixed percentage, the property owner is responsible for a proportionate share of the loss (Miller).

Incontestability clause - Some state statutes require an insurance policy for life or health insurance include an incontestability clause. These clauses restrict the ability of an insurance company to contest statements made in an application for insurance after a specified period of time, such as two or three years.

For example, in New York, an individual life insurance policy must contain a provision that the policy shall be incontestable after being in force during the life of the insured for a period of two years from its date of issue. Source: New York Insurance Law §3203.

Anti-lapse clause - This clause provides an insurance policy will not automatically lapse if payment is not made on the due date. Under this clause, an insured has a grace period to pay the overdue premium before the policy is canceled.

Appraisal clause - If an insurance company and an insured cannot agree on the amount of a loss covered under a policy – or the value of any property lost – this clause allows for either party to demand an appraisal or estimate prepared by an impartial third-party.

Arbitration clause - An arbitration clause in an insurance policy provides for disputes between the parties to an insurance policy to resolve the dispute by arbitration instead of a civil claim or lawsuit.

Multiple insurance policies - If an insured has multiple insurance policies covering the same property and the amount of coverage exceeds any loss, many policies require the loss be shared proportionally by all the insurance companies.

Defenses against payment to the insured - An insurance policy is subject to any defense that can be raised in a contract action. In addition, there are defenses available specific to an insurance contract, including:

1. Fraud of misrepresentation - If an insurance company can show the policy was obtained by fraud, it may be a valid defense to prevent payment on a claim.

2. Lack of an insurable interest - If an insurance company can show an insured did not have an insurable interest, it would be an absolute defense to a claim and the policy would be considered void right from the time it was issued.

3. Illegal actions of the insured.

Types of Life Insurance

With life insurance, an insurance company agrees to pay a sum certain on the policy to a designated person (**beneficiary**) when the insured dies. The goal of the insured in obtaining this form of insurance is to protect and provide for the beneficiary. There are generally three forms of life insurance.

1. *Term life policy* - A **term life policy** is an insurance contract in which the insurer assumes the risk of the death of the insured for a specific time with no cash surrender or value. The term of the policy may be anywhere from one, five, or ten years, or until the insured reaches the age of 65 or 70. If the insured dies during those times, the insurance company pays the face value of the policy; however, if the insured is still alive at the end of the specified term, the policy expires and coverage ends.

   Term insurance may be renewable at the end of each term; however, the premium will be higher because the insured is older and the risk of death greater. Insurance companies typically do not offer term insurance when an insured reaches the age of 65 or 70. Term life is a relatively inexpensive form of insurance because it has a set term and does not build any cash value. One benefit of a term life policy is they may be converted in some cases to a whole life policy.

2. *Whole life policy* - A **whole life policy** is an insurance contract that covers an insured for life and accumulates a cash surrender value. Premiums remain the same throughout the life of the insured and are determined based on the gender, age, health, and occupation of the insured at the time the policy is procured.

   One important feature of a whole life policy is its cash value. One portion of the premium is used to pay for insurance protection, and the other portion is deposited in a savings fund. The amount paid into the savings fund is known as the cash value, and that value grows with each premium payment.

3. *Universal life policy* - A **universal life** policy is an insurance contract that combines features of both whole life and term life policies. Accordingly, an insured can change the premium payments, face value, and period of coverage, and any premiums paid that exceed the current cost of term insurance are deposited into a savings fund and earn interest.

Funeral Home Insurance Needs

General liability insurance - This type of insurance covers a funeral home in the event a lawsuit or claim is filed alleging personal injury or property damage, e.g., slip/trip/falls on the property or in the facilities. Coverage will usually pay the legal expenses to defend a suit or claim, in addition to paying any civil judgment against the establishment up to the amount of the policy limits.

There are some insurance policies – depending on the specific company – that may cover funeral expenses if an injury results in death They may also provide coverage for loss of services and medical expenses. General liability insurance is common for a funeral home, as it covers legal costs regardless of which party is at fault or has the most liability.

Commercial property insurance - This insurance protects the funeral home facilities and business property against loss from vandalism, fire, water, and wind damage.

Funeral director's professional liability insurance - Professional **malpractice** insurance is also referred to as Errors and Omissions insurance. This pays for providing a legal defense, court costs, and any judgments obtained against a funeral director or a funeral establishment.

Commercial auto insurance - This insurance coverage protects the business and staff members in the event of a motor vehicle accident. Coverage usually includes liability and property damage, vehicle repairs, and medical expenses for injured persons.

Workers' compensation insurance - This coverage pays the cost of medical care for funeral establishment employees injured in the workplace or suffering a work-related illness. It may include payment for lost wages and other employment benefits.

Insurance options vary by state, and funeral establishment owners should periodically review coverage with an insurance broker or agent.

Glossary

Note: For information on bracketed sources, e.g., [FSL term], see chapter titled, *Book Introduction.*

Acceptance - an agreement to an offer resulting in a contract. (Chapter 4)

Accord and satisfaction - an agreement made and executed in satisfaction of the rights one has from a previous contract. (Chapter 6)

Adjudicate - the process of rendering a formal decision or judgment in a matter that is in dispute or adversarial in nature [by Author]. (Chapter 2)

Administrative agency - a governmental body created by legislation empowered to make and enforce rules and regulations [FSL term]. (Chapter 1)

Administrative law - the rules and regulations created by Federal and State administrative agencies [FSL term]. (Chapter 1)

Agent - the party appointed by the principal to enter into a contract with a third party on behalf 8 of the principal. (Chapter 14)

Alien corporation - one that is incorporated in a foreign country. (Chapter 16)

Answer - official document responding to the plaintiff's complaint. (Chapter 3)

Antitrust law - laws which seek to promote competition among businesses. (Chapter 10)

Apparent authority - the authority an agent is believed by third parties to have because of the principal's behavior. (Chapter 14)

Appeal - request to a higher court to review a lower court's decision. (Chapter 3)

Appellate courts - courts hearing cases appealed from a lower court. (Chapter 3)

Assignee - the party to whom the assignment is made. (Chapter 6)

Assignment - a means whereby one party in a contract conveys rights to another party, who is not a party to the original contract. (Chapter 6)

Assignor - the party making the assignment. (Chapter 6)

Authority - power to act for someone else. (Chapter 14)

Bailee - the party who acquires possession, but not the title, of another's personal property, under agreement. (Chapters 18 and 19)

Bailment - the transfer of possession, but not the title of another's personal property, under agreement. (Chapter 18)

Bailor - the party who gives up possession, but not the title, of personal property in a bailment. (Chapter 18)

Bearer - a person in possession of a negotiable instrument. (Chapter 11)

Bearer paper - negotiable instrument payable to bearer or cash. (Chapters 11 and 12)

Beneficiary - recipient of the proceeds of a life insurance policy. (Chapter 19)

Bilateral contract - a contract which consists of mutual promises to perform future acts. (Chapter 4)

Bill of lading - the contract existing between the consignor and the carrier. (Chapter 8)

Bill of sale - a document that conveys or evidences title to tangible personal property. (Chapters 7 and 8)

Blank indorsement - having no words other than the signature of the indorser. (Chapter 12)

Board of directors - a body of persons elected by the stockholders to define and establish corporate policy. (Chapter 16)

Breach of contract - failure or refusal to perform contractual obligations. (Chapters 6 and 15)

Business law - rules of conduct for the performance of business transactions. (Chapter 2)

Case law - appellate court decisions based on custom and usage and prior decisions [FSL term]. (Chapters 1 and 2)

Cashier's check - a check drawn on a bank's own funds and signed by a responsible bank official. (Chapter 11)

Certificate of deposit (CD) - the acknowledgment by a bank of a receipt of money with an agreement of repayment. (Chapter 11)

Certified check - a check for which the bank assures that the drawer has sufficient funds to make payment. (Chapter 11)

Check - an order by a depositor on the bank to pay a sum of money to a payee. (Chapter 11)

Civil law - the body of law concerned with private or purely personal rights. (Chapter 2)

Close (closely held) corporation - a corporation in which outstanding shares of stock and managerial control are held by a limited number of people (often members of the same family). (Chapter 16)

Common carrier - any carrier required by law to convey passengers or freight without refusal if the approved fare or charge is paid (airline, train, etc.). (Chapters 8 and 18)

Common law - the body of law deriving from judicial decisions, rather than from statutes or constitutions. (Chapters 1 and 2)

Compensatory damages - an award paid to the injured party to cover the exact amount of their loss but no more. (Chapter 6)

Complaint (petition) - the document which initiates a civil lawsuit. (Chapter 3)

Consideration - the bargained-for exchange in a contract. (Chapter 4 and 12)

Consignee - one who receives goods shipped by common carrier. (Chapter 8)

Consignor - one who ships goods by common carrier. (Chapter 8)

Constitution - the fundamental law that establishes the government; limits what government can and cannot do; and states the underlying principles to which the government will conform [FSL term]. (Chapter 1)

Contract - a legally enforceable agreement. (Chapters 4, 5, and 15)

Contract to sell - a contract to sell goods at a future time. (Chapter 7)

Contractual capacity - the legal ability to enter into a contract. (Chapter 4)

Corporation - a business entity created by statutory law and owned by individuals known as shareholders. (Chapter 16)

Counteroffer - a change to an original offer that in effect, rejects that offer and becomes a new offer. (Chapter 5)

Creditor - a person or entity to whom money is owed [by Author]. (Chapters 5 and 8)

Creditor beneficiary - a third party beneficiary owed a debt by a party to a contract. (Chapter 6)

Crime - an offense which is injurious to society as a whole. (Chapters 2 and 6)

Criminal law - laws dealing with crimes and the punishment of wrongdoers. (Chapter 2)

Debtor - a person or entity that owes money to another [by Author]. (Chapters 17)

Deed - document conveying title to real property. (Chapters 17 and 18)

Defendant - the party against whom legal action is brought. (Chapter 3)

Delegation - transfer of contractual duties to a third party. (Chapter 6)

Disaffirmance - election to avoid a voidable contract. (Chapter 5)

Discharge - any method by which a legal duty is extinguished. (Chapter 6)

Discovery - the formal and informal exchange of information between sides in a lawsuit. (Chapter 3)

Dissolution - in business matters, the official act or process of formally ending the operations of an enterprise, such as a corporation [by Author]. (Chapter 15)

Domestic corporation - operates in the state that granted the charter. (Chapter 16)

Donee beneficiary - a third party beneficiary to whom no legal duty is owed and performance is a gift. (Chapter 6)

Draft - a written order by one person directing another to pay a sum of money, to a third person. (Chapters 11 and 12)

Drawee - the person, company or financial institution ordered to pay a draft. (Chapters 11 and 12)

Drawer - the person who executes any draft. (Chapters 11 and 12)

Durable power of attorney - A power of attorney that remains in effect after the disability or incapacity of the principal [FSL term]. (Chapter 14)

Duress - removing one's free will and obtaining consent by means of a threat. (Chapter 6)

Employee - a person hired to perform work that is directed and controlled by the employer. (Chapter 13)

Employer - the party who employs employees to do certain work. (Chapter 13)

Executed contract - a contract in which the terms have been fulfilled. (Chapter 4)

Execution - the carrying out or completion of some task. (Chapter 3)

Executory contract - a contract in which the terms have not been completely executed or fulfilled. (Chapter 4)

Existing goods - goods which are, at the time of the contract, in existence and owned by the seller. (Chapter 7)

Express authority - authority of an agent, stated in the agreement creating the agency. (Chapter 14)

Express contract - a contract in which the parties express their intentions, either verbally or in writing, at the time of the agreement. (Chapter 4)

Express warranty - the actual and definite statement of a seller, either verbally or in writing, at the time of the sale. (Chapter 8)

Fee simple estate - the broadest form of ownership in real property. (Chapter 17)

Felony - serious criminal offense punishable by imprisonment for more than one year or death. (Chapter 2)

Fiduciary - a person in a relationship of trust and confidence. (Chapters 4, 6 and 14)

Fixture - objects permanently attached to land. (Chapter 18)

Foreign corporation - a corporation that operates in a state other than where it is chartered. (Chapter 16)

Fraud - inducing another to contract as a result of an intentionally or recklessly false statement of a material fact. (Chapter 6)

Funeral service law (mortuary law/mortuary jurisprudence) - that branch of law which relates to matters concerned with the disposal of the dead and regulation of funeral directors, embalmers, and funeral establishments [FSL term]. (Chapter 1)

Future goods - goods not in existence or not yet owned by the seller at the time the contract was created. (Chapter 7)

General agent - one who is given broad authority to conduct the principal's business. (Chapter 14)

General partner - individual actively and openly engaged in the business and held to everyone as a partner. (Chapter 15)

General Power of Attorney - A written instrument granting the agent broad powers to act for the principal [FSL term]. (Chapter 14)

Goods - movable tangible personal property. (Chapter 7)

Gross negligent act - the intentional failure or the reckless disregard of the consequences with respect to conduct affecting the life or property of another [FSL term]. (Chapter 18)

Holder - one in possession of a negotiable instrument. (Chapter 12)

Identified goods - the goods specified by the buyer and seller. (Chapter 7)

Impeach - call into question the integrity or validity of (a practice) [Oxford Dictionary]. (Chapter 3)

Implied authority - an agent's authority to do things in order to carry out express authority. (Chapters 8 and 14)

Implied contract - one in which the terms of the contract are implied by acts or conduct of the parties. (Chapter 4)

Implied warranties - warranties imposed by law, arising automatically because the sale has been made. (Chapter 8)

Indemnification - a legal agreement by one party to hold another party not liable for potential losses or damages [CRM term]. (Chapters 14 and 19)

Independent contractor - one who contracts to do jobs and is controlled only by the contract as to how performance is to be rendered. (Chapter 13)

Indorsee - named holder of indorsed negotiable instrument. (Chapter 12)

Indorsement - signature of holder on the back of a negotiable instrument, with any directions or limitations. (Chapter 12)

Indorser - person who signs his or her name on back of an instrument. (Chapter 12)

Injunction - a judicial order or decree forbidding certain conduct. (Chapter 6)

Intangible personal property -personal property that lacks a physical presence. (Chapter 7)

Judgment - a decision of a court. (Chapter 3)

Jurisdiction - the official power to make legal decisions and judgments [Oxford Dictionary]. (Chapter 3)

Law - governmental rule prescribing conduct and carrying a penalty for violation. (Chapters 2 and 2)

Liability - responsibility for actions and/or other debts; the quality or state of being legally obligated or accountable [FSL term]. (Chapters 15 and 18)

Life estate - interest in real property for duration of a person's life. (Chapter 17)

Limited liability company (LLC) - hybrid form of business organization that combines features of both a corporation and partnership. (Chapter 15)

Limited partner - partner whose liability for the firm's debts is limited to the amount of his or her investment. (Chapter 15)

Liquidated damages - damages stipulated in a contract to be paid in the event of a breach. (Chapter 6)

Maker - the party who executes a promissory note. (Chapters 11 and 12)

Malpractice - failure to perform a professional service with the ability and care generally exercised by others in the profession. (Chapter 19)

Merchant - a person who deals in goods of the kind, or otherwise by occupation purports to have knowledge or skill peculiar to the practices or goods involved in the transaction. (Chapters 7 and 8)

Minor - those persons under legal age; for most states, the standard is under the age of eighteen. (Chapter 5)

Misdemeanor - a less serious crime punishable by fine and/or imprisonment of less than one year. (Chapter 2)

Misrepresentation - false statement of a material fact. (Chapter 6)

Mortgage - a secured loan on a parcel of real property [FSL term]. (Chapters 17 and 19)

Necessaries - items required for living at a reasonable standard (i.e. food, clothing and shelter). (Chapter 5)

Negligence - failure to exercise reasonable care. (Chapters 2 and 17)

Negotiable instrument - a writing drawn in a special form which can be transferred as a substitute for money or as an instrument of credit. (Chapter 11)

Negotiation - the act of transferring ownership of a negotiable instrument to another party. (Chapters 11 and 12)

Nominal damages - small amount awarded when there is a technical breach but no injury. (Chapter 6)

Note - a promise to pay money [by Author]. (Chapter 12)

Novation - the substitution of a new party for one of the original parties to a contract, such that the prior contract terminates and a new one substitutes for it. (Chapter 6)

Offer - a proposal to make a contract. (Chapter 4)

Offeree - the party to whom an offer is made. (Chapter 5)

Offeror - the party who initiates or makes an offer. (Chapter 5)

Order paper - negotiable instrument made payable to the order of a named party; the word 'order' or its equivalent must be used. (Chapters 11 and 12)

Ordinance - law enacted by a local unit of government. (Chapter 1)

Partnership - the voluntary association of two or more people who have combined their resources to carry on as co-owners a lawful enterprise for their joint profit. (Chapter 15)

Payee - the party to whom a negotiable instrument is made payable. (Chapters 11 and 12)

Perjury - offense of willfully telling an untruth in a court after having taken an oath or affirmation [Oxford Dictionary]. (Chapter 3)

Personal property - all property which is not real property. (Chapters 7, 17 and 18)

Petition - see Complaint. (Chapter 3)

Plaintiff - the party who initiates a civil action. (Chapter 3)

Police power - the inherent power of a government to make reasonable laws to protect the safety, health, morals, and general welfare of its citizens [FSL term]. (Chapters 1 and 2)

Power of attorney - An instrument granting someone authority to act as agent or attorney-in-fact for the principal; an ordinary power of attorney is revocable and automatically terminates upon the death or incapacity of the principal [FSL term]. (Chapter 14)

Price - the consideration stipulated by contract, generally expressed in money. (Chapter 7)

Principal - a party who appoints another to serve as an agent. (Chapter 14)

Private carrier - those who transport only in particular instances and only for those they chose to contract with (e.g., funeral establishment vehicles and livery). (Chapter 8)

Private corporation - a corporation formed to carry out some non-governmental function. (Chapter 16)

Probate court - a court having jurisdiction over estates [FSL term]. (Chapter 3)

Promissory estoppel - an equitable doctrine that prevents the promisor from revoking the promise when the promisee justifiably acts in reliance upon the promise to his or her detriment. (Chapters 5 and 7)

Promissory note - a negotiable instrument containing a promise to pay. (Chapters 11 and 12)

Promoter - a person or entity that acts on behalf of a corporation to devise and implement a plan for its formation [by Author]. (Chapter 16)

Public corporation - a corporation formed to carry out government functions. (Chapter 16)

Punitive damages - an award paid to the plaintiff in order to punish the defendant. (Chapter 6)

Qualified indorsement - an indorsement which limits the liability of the indorser. (Chapter 12)

Quasi contract - a contract created or implied by law to prevent unjust enrichment. (Chapter 4)

Ratification - approving an act which was executed without authority; electing to be bound by a voidable contract. (Chapter 5)

Real property - land and those objects permanently attached to land. (Chapters 4, 7, 17 and 18)

Rescission - to set aside or cancel a contract. (Chapter 6)

Rejection - refusal to accept. (Chapter 5)

Restrictive indorsement - indorsement that restricts use of a negotiable instrument. (Chapter 12)

Revocation - cancellation of an instrument by the maker or drawer; rescinding an offer. (Chapter 5)

Rules and regulations - laws created by an administrative agency within its jurisdiction [FSL term]. (Chapter 1)

Salary - Generally considered to be compensation for managerial or administrative services expressed in terms of a month or year [SBM term]. (Chapter 13)

Sale - the transfer of title to goods from the seller to the buyer for consideration. (Chapter 7)

Secured claim - a debt which is supported by a pledge, mortgage or lien on assets belonging to the debtor [FSL term]. (Chapter 17)

Service contract - a contract whose subject matter predominantly involves services. (Chapters 7 and 8)

Shareholders (stockholders) - see Stockholders. (Chapter 16)

Sherman Antitrust Act - federal legislation intended to promote competition among businesses by prohibiting restraint of trade. (Chapter 10)

Silent partner - an individual who takes no active part in the management of a partnership, but has capital invested in the business. (Chapter 15)

Sole proprietorship - a business owned by one person, who is personally subject to claims of creditors. (Chapter 15)

Special agent - one authorized by the principal to execute specific act(s). (Chapter 14)

Special indorsement - an indorsement which designates the particular person to whom payment is to be made. (Chapter 12)

Specific performance - a remedy by which the court requires the breaching party to perform the contract. (Chapter 6)

Springing power of attorney - A written instrument authorizing one person to act as an agent for another effective only upon a certain event occurring [FSL term]. (Chapter 14)

Stare decisis - the principle that the decision of a higher court should serve as a guide or precedent and control the decision of a similar case in the future. (Chapter 1)

Statement of Funeral Goods and Services Selected - an itemized list of goods and services that a consumer has selected during an arrangement conference that allows them to evaluate the selections and make any desired changes [FTC Guide, pg. 15]. (Chapter 18)

Statute of Frauds - law requiring certain contracts be in writing to be enforceable. (Chapters 4 and 14)

Statute of limitations - a law that restricts the period of time within which an action may be brought to court. (Chapters 5 and 6)

Statutes - laws which are enacted by legislative bodies. (Chapters 1 and 2)

Stockholders (shareholders) - those having title to one or more shares of stock in a corporation; combined, they represent ownership of the corporation. (Chapter 16)

Subchapter S corporation - business organization in which shareholders are taxed as a partnership (no double taxation) without losing corporation status. (Chapter 16)

Summons - a notice given to a defendant, attaching the complaint and stating a time frame in which to respond. (Chapter 3)

Term life policy - contract whereby insurer assumes risk of death of insured for a specific time with no cash surrender value. (Chapter 19)

Third party beneficiary - person not party to a contract, but whom parties intended to benefit. (Chapter 6)

Title - ownership; evidence of ownership of property. (Chapters 7, 8 and 18)

Tort - a private or civil wrong against a person or his or her property, other than by breach of contract, for which there may be action for damages. (Chapters 2, 6 and 15)

Trial court - court which conducts the original trial of a case. (Chapter 3)

Undue influence - improper influence that is asserted by one dominant person over another, without the threat of harm. (Chapter 6)

Unenforceable contract - an agreement which at the current time is not enforceable by law. (Chapter 4)

Uniform Commercial Code (UCC) - model act that includes provisions concerning certain sales of goods and negotiable instruments. (Chapters 4, 5, 7, 8 and 12)

Unilateral contract - a contract formed when an act is done in consideration for a promise. (Chapter 4)

Universal life policy - an insurance product combining features of both whole life and term life policies. (Chapter 19)

Usurious - exceeding the maximum rate of interest which may be charged on loans. (Chapters 6 and 10)

Valid contract - a contract which is legally enforceable. (Chapters 4 and 5)

Void contract - an agreement of no legal effect. (Chapters 4 and 5)

Voidable contract - a contract which would be an enforceable agreement, but due to circumstances may be set aside by one of the parties. (Chapters 4 and 5)

W-2 form - Wage and tax statement; a report furnished by the employer for each employee indicating gross earnings and deductions [SBM term]. (Chapter 13)

Wage - A form of compensation usually for skilled and unskilled labor expressed in terms of hours, weeks or pieces completed [SBM term]. (Chapter 13)

Warranties - guarantees made by a seller that an article, good or service will conform to a certain standard or will operate in a certain manner. (Chapter 8)

Whole life policy - insurance that covers an insured for life and accumulates cash surrender value. (Chapter 19)

Sources Consulted

American Bar Association. "How Courts Work." Division of Public Education, Chicago, Illinois; retrieved December 2020.
URL: https://www.americanbar.org/groups/public_education/resources/law_related_education_network/how_courts_work

American Board of Funeral Service Education. "Business Law." Curriculum outline as approved in April 2018.

Ashcroft, John, et al. *Law for Business, 19th ed.* Boston Massachusetts: Cengage Learning, 2019.

Balsiger Insurance. "Funeral Home Insurance".
URL: https://balsigerinsurance.com/funeral-home-insurance?

Black's Law Dictionary - *See entry: Garner, Bryan A.*

Burnham, Scott. *Contract Law for Dummies.* Hoboken, NJ: John Wiley & Sons, Inc., 2012.

Chen, James. "Note." Investopedia, Dotdash Publishing, New York, NY, updated January 17, 2021; retrieved January 2022.
URL: https://www.investopedia.com/terms/n/note.asp

---. "Statute of Frauds." Investopedia, Dotdash Publishing, New York, NY, updated March 14, 2021; retrieved August 2021.
URL: https://www.investopedia.com/terms/s/statute-of-frauds.asp

Cleveland, Larry J. *Funeral Service Law in the United States, 2nd ed.* Hudson Valley Professional Services, 2021.

Emerson, Robert W. *Business Law, 6th ed.* Kaplan Inc, d/b/a Barron's Educational Series, New York, NY, 2015.

Fleischer, Charles H. *The SHRM Essential Guide to Employment Law A Handbook for HR Professionals, Managers, Businesses and Organizations, 1st ed.* Society for Human Resource Management, Alexandria, VA, 2018

Folger, Jean. "Real Property." Investopedia, Dotdash Publishing, New York, NY, updated December 7, 2020; retrieved January 2021.
URL: https://www.investopedia.com/terms/r/real-property.asp

Garner, Bryan A., and Henry Campbell Black. *Black's Law Dictionary 11th ed.* St. Paul, MN, Thomson Reuters, 2019.

Goldman, Arnold J., and William D. Sigismond. *Business Law Principles and Practices*, 8th editon. Mason Ohio: South-Western Cengage Learning, 2011.

Hayes, Adam. "Shareholder." Investopedia, Dotdash Publishing, New York, NY, updated June 20, 2020; retrieved January 2021.
URL: https://www.investopedia.com/terms/s/shareholder.asp

HG.org Legal Resources. "Infamous Antitrust Cases." Retrieved September 2021.
URL: https://www.hg.org/legal-articles/infamous-antitrust-cases-6025

Jaeger-Fine, Toni M. *American Legal Systems: A Resource and Reference Book, 3rd ed.* Carolina Academic Press, Durham, North Carolina, 2020.

Kagan, Julie. "Bank Draft." Investopedia, Dotdash Publishing, New York, NY, updated October 30, 2020; retrieved January 2022.
URL: https://www.investopedia.com/terms/b/bank_draft.asp

---. "Fiduciary." Investopedia, Dotdash Publishing, New York, NY, updated October 22, 2020; retrieved January 2021.
URL: https://www.investopedia.com/terms/f/fiduciary.asp.

---. "Personal Property." Investopedia, Dotdash Publishing, New York, NY, updated September 11, 2019; retrieved January 2021.
URL: https://www.investopedia.com/terms/p/personal-property.asp

Kenton, Will. "Estoppel." Investopedia, Dotdash Publishing, New York, NY, updated November 28, 2020; retrieved February 2022.
URL: https://www.investopedia.com/terms/e/estoppel.asp

Kubasak, Michael, and William M. Lamers. *Traversing the Minefield Best Practice: Reducing Risk in Funeral-Cremation Service.* Malibu, California: LMG Publishing, 2007.

Legal Information Institute. "Parol Evidence Rule." Cornell Law School; Cornell, New York; retrieved August 2021.
URL: https://www.law.cornell.edu/wex/parol_evidence_rule

---. "Tort." Cornell Law School; Cornell, New York; retrieved January 2021.
URL: https://www.law.cornell.edu/wex/tort

Legal Information Institute. "Vicarious Liability." Cornell Law School; Cornell, New York; retrieved February 2022.
URL: https://www.law.cornell.edu/wex/vicarious_liability

Liberto, Daniel. "Quasi-Public Corporation." Investopedia, Dotdash Publishing, New York, NY, updated August 26, 2019; retrieved January 2021.
URL: https://www.investopedia.com/terms/q/quasi_public_corporation.asp.

Liuzzo, Anthony. *Essentials of Business Law, 9th ed.* New York, NY, McGraw-Hill Education, 2016.

Miller, Roger LeRoy. *Business Law Today: The Essentials Diverse, Ethical, Online, and Global Environment,* 10th edition. Mason, Ohio: South-Western, Cengage Learning, 2014.

Oxford University Press. "Jurisdiction." Lexico.com, 2020, retrieved January 2021.
URL: https://www.lexico.com/en/definition/jurisdiction

Patterson, T. *Business Legal Structures, 3rd ed.* (No publisher information available)

Raymond, Phil. "*Justice Department Alleges Clayton Act Antitrust Violations Against AT&T and Time Warner Merger*." Juris Magazine, Duquesne University School of Law, Pittsburgh, PA, December 2, 2017, retrieved September 2021.
URL: https://sites.law.duq.edu/juris/2017/12/02/justice-department-alleges-clayton-act-antitrust-violations-against-att-and-time-warner-merger/

Trusted Choice. "Funeral Home Insurance Lets You Stay Focused on Your Customers".
URL: https://www.trustedchoice.com/n/81/funeral-home-insurance/

United States, Department of Labor, Federal Trade Commission. "Complying with the Funeral Rule." United States Government, April 2019.

USLegal. "Remotely-Created Consumer Item Law and Legal Definition." AirSlate Legal Forms, Inc., Brookline, Massachusetts. Retrieved online January 2022.
URL: https://definitions.uslegal.com/r/remotely-created-consumer-item/

West's Encyclopedia of American Law, 2nd ed. "Answer." Thomas/Gale Publishers, Detroit, Michigan, Vol. 1 pg. 285, 2005.

---. "Bill of Lading." Thomas/Gale Publishers, Detroit, MI, Vol. 2 pg. 29, 2005.

---. "Bill of Sale." Thomas/Gale Publishers, Detroit, MI, Vol. 2 pg. 35, 2005.

---. "Civil Complaint." Thomas/Gale Publishers, Detroit, MI, Vol. 3 pg. 54, 2005.

---. "Civil Law." Thomas/Gale Publishers, Detroit, MI, Vol. 2 pg. 389, 2005.

---. "Commercial Paper." Thomas/Gale Publishers, Detroit, MI, Vol. 3, pg. 15, 2005.

---. "Common Law." Thomas/Gale Publishers, Detroit, MI, Vol. 3 pg. 30, 2005.

---. "Criminal Law." Thomas/Gale Publishers, Detroit, MI, Vol. 3 pg. 273, 2005.

---. "Consideration." Thomas/Gale Publishers, Detroit, MI, Vol. 3, pg. 105, 2005.

---. "Illusory Promise." Thomas/Gale Publishers, Detroit, MI, Vol. 5, pg. 328, 2005.

---. "Lease." Thomas/Gale Publishers, Detroit, MI, Vol. 6 pg. 223, 2005.

---. "Negotiable Instrument." Thomas/Gale Publishers, Detroit, MI, Vol. 8, pg. 228, 2005

---. "Property Law." Thomas/Gale Publishers, Detroit, MI, Vol. 8, pg. 145, 2005.

---. "Sherman Anti-trust Act." Thomas/Gale Publishers, Detroit, MI, Vol. 9, pg. 165, 2005.

---. "Holder in Due Course." Thomas/Gale Publishers, Detroit, MI, Vol. 5, pg. 273, 2005.

Whaley, Douglas J. "Commercial Paper and Payment Law." Gilbert Law Summaries, LEG, Inc. d/b/a West Academic Publishing, 2013.

---. "Sale and Lease of Goods." Gilbert Law Summaries, LEG, Inc. d/b/a West Academic Publishing, 2021.

Illustration Sources

1. **Image** - Contract
   Illustration courtesy of U.S. Army
   Retrieved online at Wikimedia Commons, August 2021
   URL: https://upload.wikimedia.org/wikipedia/commons/8/8a/ContractLaw.jpg

2. **Image** - Life Insurance Street Sign
   Illustration courtesy of Investmentzen
   Retrieved online at Flickr, October 2021
   URL: www.investmentzen.com

Index

Hudson Valley Professional Services

~ Educating the Funeral Service Industry ~